W9-CPM-648

Men I've
Never Been

LIVING OUT

Gay and Lesbian Autobiographies

DAVID BERGMAN, JOAN LARKIN, and
RAPHAEL KADUSHIN,
Founding Editors

Men I've
Never Been

Michael Sadowski

THE UNIVERSITY OF WISCONSIN PRESS

The University of Wisconsin Press
728 State Street, Suite 443
Madison, Wisconsin 53706
uwpress.wisc.edu

Gray's Inn House, 127 Clerkenwell Road
London EC1R 5DB, United Kingdom
eurospanbookstore.com

Printed in the United States of America
This book may be available in a digital edition.

Library of Congress Cataloging-in-Publication Data
Names: Sadowski, Michael, author.
Title: Men I've never been / Michael Sadowski.
Other titles: Living out.
Description: Madison, Wisconsin : The University of Wisconsin Press,
[2021] | Series: Living out: gay and lesbian autobiographies
Identifiers: LCCN 2020035741 | ISBN 9780299330903 (cloth)
Subjects: LCSH: Sadowski, Michael. | Gay men—United States—Biography.
| LCGFT: Autobiographies.
Classification: LCC HQ75.8.S23 A3 2021 | DDC 306.76/62092 [B]—dc23
LC record available at https://lccn.loc.gov/2020035741

To all my siblings,
by blood and otherwise

Contents

Author's Note

This is a work of memory. Although I have consulted with family members and friends to check my recollection of various facts, this book represents interpretations and opinions that are solely my own. It is based on true events, but I have reconstructed scenes, dialogue, and other details with the goal of rendering what I remember, and especially how I remember it, as faithfully as possible. Many conversations depicted in this book also contain what I call "anchor lines," statements that I recall verbatim. I would bet my life on the accuracy of these words. There are no composite characters, but the names and identifying details of many people and locations have been changed in the interest of anonymity.

BEFORE

The Professor

Before all the times I failed at being a man, I succeeded at being a professor. Or at least that's what my father said.

In my second-earliest memory, he and I are on a mystery drive in his sky blue Galaxie 500. It's July, or maybe August, 1966, before most cars had air-conditioning. The windows are wide open, and a sickly sweet, medicinal odor wafts in with the summer heat. Peeking over the dashboard, I can see the looming stacks of a chemical factory churning out plumes of pink and silver smoke. Then we pull into a gravel parking lot, a cloud of gray dust kicking up under our wheels.

"Where are we?"

My father's only answer: a wide, toothy grin.

With no seatbelt to undo, I tumble easily out of the passenger seat, and we walk toward a flat-roofed, one-story structure identified only by a black, hand-painted road sign I can more or less sound out as "Club Royale." As I would later find out, Club Royale was one of the many places my father frequented that my mother wouldn't dignify with the word "bar." To her, places of this ilk were "beer joints," dumps she wouldn't be caught dead in under any circumstances.

The inside of Club Royale is dark, impenetrable to my four-year-old eyes, and it smells like that combination of stale beer, cork, and old tobacco smoke that permeates dive bars and low-end fraternity houses everywhere. Right away, it's clear that my father has a following here. From the moment we walk in, people start waving and calling out *John this!* and *John that!*, which seems strange to me. I'd always heard people call my father Yosh (rhymes with Josh), a Polish nickname from my immigrant grandmother that stuck with the rest of the family. But here, he's John, and everybody loves him. That seems a little strange to me, too.

Between my parents, my father was decidedly the extrovert. With wavy brown hair only starting to gray at forty-eight, pale green eyes, and a ready smile, Yosh was at his best with casual acquaintances. He would often get into angry tussles with strangers about their lousy driving, how long they took with the bank teller while he waited in line, or the price of an item he thought was too high. To my mother and my six older siblings, he was a serial disappointment—never following through on plans, never showing up when he said he'd give them a ride, or if he did show up, never arriving sober. But to the regulars at his beer joints, people who knew his name but not much else, my father was friendly and funny, a great guy to have around.

"Whoa, John! Haven't see ya here in a while! How ya been?"

After acknowledging the greetings of his admirers, Yosh sits me up on a barstool and grabs a copy of the *Daily News*, a working-class New York tabloid that probably could have been found in every other beer joint in central Jersey. He holds it up high so that the widest possible audience can see it.

"Hey! Hey! Lookit!" Yosh shouts, trying to capture the attention of the entire room. Then he barks, "Michael!" He sounds like he's furious, but I've heard this tone before, so I know what he's up to. "Whazzit say on that paper?"

Falling right into my father's trap, some incredulous barfly pipes up, "That little kid? He can't read that!"

"Wanna bet?" Then another bark from Yosh, this one even louder and angrier-sounding than the first: "Michael! Whazzit say?"

Slowly sounding out the headlines in block letters that are a trademark of the *Daily News* front page to this day, I intone haltingly, but mostly accurately, headlines like:

THE BLACKOUT: NOBODY DIGS POWER FLOP

THREE SLAIN. BOMB RIPS SAY . . . SAY-GONE

This being near the height of the Vietnam War, the headlines often include the names of places and political figures I stumble on. But do my father's cronies at Club Royale know the difference? And even if some do, sounding out "say-gone" for Saigon is still pretty good for a kid who's not even in preschool.

"John, I'm gonna buy you a drink!" says one new believer, then another. Yosh opens up the paper, and the game continues with page 4, page 7, the back-page sports news. The more headlines I read, the more beer and whiskey my father gets for free.

"What'll you have, John?"

"Shot and a beer." Over and over.

I probably get free Cokes out of the bets, too. I don't remember, though many decades later I can recall quite clearly the location of the men's room at Club Royale, so I must have been taking in a fair amount of liquid myself.

After an hour or two, my father and I walk out of Club Royale and back into the hot summer sun, the chemical odor from across the highway now tinged with the sweet smell of victory. Then we spin out of the gravel parking lot and drive home, leaving only wonderment and a cloud of gray dust behind us.

～

"You took him to a *beer joint*? In the middle of the *afternoon*? What the hell's wrong with you?"

I don't recall a single instance of my parents ever speaking lovingly to one another. Whatever tenderness might have once existed between Yosh and Sophie, the head-turningly handsome couple in the Niagara Falls honeymoon portrait that now sat unframed and wrinkled in our family photo box—Yosh in his green Army uniform and Sophie with the long brown hair, brown eyes, and aquiline nose of a strong-willed 1940s movie heroine—it was long gone by the time their seventh child came along. So I was neither surprised nor troubled by Sophie's reaction when Yosh, too many shots and beers in him to know better, bragged about the feat we had just pulled off at Club Royale.

"He was readin'! Outta the paper! Those guys there, they couldn't believe it!" he answered with a gassy smile, obviously tone-deaf to what my mother thought of all this. "I tell ya, Soph, that kid can read!"

"Yeah? I'll read *you*!" This was one of Sophie's favorite comebacks in her exchanges with Yosh: take a verb he had just used and turn it on him as a threat, albeit a nonsensical one.

I don't remember what happened next. In all likelihood, realizing she would get nowhere with Yosh in his state of loopy oblivion, Sophie just sighed, rolled her eyes, and walked away. What I do remember is that my father loved the Club Royale story and retold it on many occasions, prophetically referring to me in it as "the professor" whenever he did. Always a man of stock tales and signature catchphrases, Yosh incorporated the line "John, I'm gonna buy you a drink!" into his regular repertoire. And whenever I heard it, I swelled with pride knowing I was exactly the boy my father wanted me to be.

~

My first memory, even earlier than the one at Club Royale, is of another game show in which I am the sole contestant and undefeated champion.

This time, the set is a tiny kitchen on Lincoln Avenue in Somerville, the center of central New Jersey. The walls are in wood paneling the color of honey, and a framed replica of *The Last Supper* hangs on the wall behind the studio audience: Sophie, Yosh, my three brothers, and my three sisters, all sitting around a sparkly gold Formica table. The emcee, my fifteen-year-old brother Larry, is firing out the questions, and I'm firing back the answers without missing a beat.

"How much is two and two?"

"Four!"

"How much is four and four?"

"Eight!"

"How much is eight and eight?"

"Sixteen!"

This doubling sequence I had memorized—there was no real addition involved—continues all the way up to:

"How much is two thousand forty-eight and two thousand forty-eight?"

"Four thousand ninety-six!"

Then cheers, laughter, and applause—all of it for me.

~

Every so often I'm asked—maybe in a writing workshop, maybe before going under anesthesia—to close my eyes, take myself back to a favorite place, and bask in the warmth of the feelings it evokes. I don't go to a sundrenched beach in the Caribbean or to a hammock on a spring afternoon. Instead, I go back more than fifty years to that little kitchen or sometimes that seedy bar. Back to a time when all it took to be the boy everyone cheered for was the right answer. Back before I started school, when knowing the right answer could bring either praise from the teacher or taunts from the other boys in class. Back before my father started disappearing a lot and my parents' arguing turned to shouting, then pushing and shoving, then something even worse. Back before my siblings started disappearing from the house, too, one by one. Back before I had any idea what it meant to be a man or even a boy. Back before it all felt impossible to escape, no matter how old I grew, what I accomplished, or how far I ran.

PART ONE

NOISE

I remember the gleams and glooms that dart
Across the school-boy's brain;
The song and the silence in the heart,
That in part are prophecies, and in part
Are longings wild and vain.

—HENRY WADSWORTH LONGFELLOW

When someone with the authority of a teacher, say, describes the world and you are not in it, there is a moment of psychic disequilibrium, as if you looked in the mirror and saw nothing.

—ADRIENNE RICH

Benny and me in front of our house. My best guess is that he's in third grade here and I'm in first.

I

Schoolboy

My kindergarten teacher was Mrs. Clark and my first-grade teacher was Miss Langer. But my first *real* teacher, the one who schooled me in the ways of the world and how I should and shouldn't move through it, was Sheila Feldman.

If a casting director had been scouting Van Derveer Elementary School for a live-action *Peanuts* movie, Sheila Feldman would have been flown to Hollywood to read for the role of Peppermint Patty—shoulder-length, dishwater-brown hair, parted on the side and in need of a shampoo; pale, freckled skin; and a boy's shirt three sizes too big. Her voice had that same sandpapery timbre, too, like she was talking and clearing phlegm from her throat at the same time. Ultimately, though, I don't think Sheila would have gotten the role. Because where Peppermint Patty always had that chummy sweetness, trying to buck up Charlie Brown when he thought the whole world was against him, Sheila Feldman's way of dealing with a misfit boy was entirely different.

Always referred to by both her first and last names, Sheila Feldman already had a reputation by the age of five. There were only two kindergarten teachers at Van Derveer: my teacher, the young, pretty Mrs. Clark, and Sheila's teacher, the grandmotherly Mrs. Batterly. Their rooms were adjacent to one another, and peeking through the pass-through doorway, my classmates would whisper and point. "Uh-oh, there's Sheila Feldman. Sheila Feldman's in trouble again. Did you hear what Sheila Feldman called Mrs. Batterly? She made her teacher cry. You better stay away from Sheila Feldman!" So I tried—and managed to— throughout kindergarten.

Sheila Feldman wasn't in my first-grade class either, but that fall I saw her almost every morning. Before school she would hang out by the main facade of the building, where a row of leafy bushes grew, and scowl at passersby. I felt sorry for Sheila because no one, not even the teachers, seemed to like her. And since we knew each other a little from the year before, when the kindergarten classes had combined for special activities, I'd say a tentative "hi, Sheila" whenever I saw her. She'd say "hi" back in a low, gravelly monosyllable I found hard to read. Was she surprised I knew who she was? Was she mad at me for bothering her? Or did she think it was nice that at least somebody—a boy, no less—was paying attention to her?

One morning I was walking toward A-9, my first-grade classroom. I felt relieved not to see Sheila loitering in her usual spot. Then, seemingly out of nowhere, she popped out and dragged me behind the bushes. Despite the fact that she was about the same size as me, Sheila was incredibly strong and obviously very determined. It went down something like this:

"You want to fight? I'm gonna fight you!" Sheila said.

This made no sense to me.

"Fight? I don't want to fight! What do you mean?"

"Why are you always *talkin'* to me?"

"I don't know!"

("Because no one likes you and I feel sorry for you" seemed *not* the right thing to say at that moment.)

Sheila grabbed at my shirt and pulled at my hair. It stung.

"What are you, scared?" she asked.

"I'm not scared! I just don't want to fight a *girl*."

"*You're* a girl! No—you're a sissy, that's what you are. A little sissy boy. Sissy! Sissy! Sissssssyyyyy!"

Next, a kick in the shin, then a hard punch in the gut.

"What did I *do*?" I asked, flabbergasted and—by now—on the ground.

But I got no answer. Once Sheila achieved her apparent goal of dragging, punching, and kicking me into a state of stunned humiliation, she ran away. Maybe she saw a teacher coming, maybe she was exasperated that I wasn't fighting back. Despite Sheila's brutish behavior, I just couldn't bring myself to hit a girl. In fact, I couldn't imagine hitting or wanting to hit anybody.

I came out from behind the bushes and cleaned the mulch off my clothes as best I could. I was relieved not to see Sheila or anyone else looking at me or, worse, laughing. But as I walked toward Miss Langer's room, I started adding some things up.

I thought about story time—how when I read aloud I'd sometimes get too excited, wave my hands, let my voice go up to a pitch that made other kids snicker and Miss Langer stifle a nervous laugh. Then I thought about arts and crafts, when I'd obsess over whether to use aquamarine or teal to paint my plaster of Paris horse. Then I thought back to kindergarten, when I wanted to cook imaginary dinners in the Susie Homemaker kitchen instead of building houses and bridges with Lincoln Logs, like all the other boys in the opposite corner of the room. (I made that mistake only once, the day Charlene Miller told me that the kitchen was for girls and I should get out.) And I started to wonder if maybe it was all connected.

When I reached A-9, I lined up with the other kids—the word "sissy" still playing on a continuous loop inside my head—and said nothing. Admitting to my classmates that I'd just gotten beat up by a girl seemed like a bad idea, and telling them what she'd called me seemed like an even worse one. And I knew that what I really wanted to do—cry—was *completely* out of the question. Miss Langer was pretty nice and probably would have done something to make sure Sheila was punished if I told on her. But then what would I have become in Miss Langer's eyes? The thing Sheila said I was?

Telling my parents what happened with Sheila seemed like an even worse idea. Yosh was out at his beer joints even more often than before, except now without his headline-reading sidekick along for the ride. And when he was around, the bickering between Sophie and him had escalated to something worse.

"Get the hell away from me! You're nothin' but a goddamn drunk!"

"Bullshit! To hell with you, ya goddamn bitch!"

Shouting and cursing was now my parents' default mode of communication, as much a part of the structure of our house as the beams and the walls. But the first of their altercations that really scared me took place on a Saturday afternoon in front of the gas stove that sat in the corner of our kitchen. There, I saw the familiar shouts of goddamn this, shit that, and son of a bitch get physical—Yosh holding Sophie's wrist in a grip so tight it made the veins bulge, Sophie arming herself with a metal soup ladle, attempting to fight off Yosh with blows to the head. While Yosh staggered Sophie back toward the lit stove, its two front burners blazing, I sat in stunned silence as I pictured my mother, then the kitchen, then the entire house going up in flames.

Then there was the biggest change of all. Somehow, amid all the swearing and shoving, Sophie and Yosh were also apparently having sex, because the year I was in kindergarten my brother Thomas was born. Thomas started out like all babies—a crying, drooling blob that wasn't much of a threat to my status as pet little brother. But he grew into his blond, blue-eyed cuteness at about a year old. He started to do and say funny things, like calling Larry "La La," and before long the family galaxy had a new star.

So on the day of my big run-in with Sheila, I just followed my typical routine. I walked home for lunch, sat at the head of the gold Formica table in our kitchen, and ate my SpaghettiOs. Then I quietly stepped into the living room and sat on the opposite end of the sofa from my mother, who was humming and rocking Thomas to sleep in preparation for his afternoon nap. With the volume turned low so that I didn't wake the baby, I watched *Jeopardy!* I didn't understand most of the questions, but it was nice to know there was still a place out there where people got applause and won things just for knowing the right answers.

I saw Sheila Feldman a couple of times around school after our rumble in the bushes. She shot me a few dirty looks, mumbled a few insults. Then I didn't see her at all for what I eventually realized had been a long time. I wasn't sure if her family had moved or why she'd suddenly disappeared, but I didn't want to ask anyone for fear they'd start asking me why I cared so much.

Months went by, then years. It was pretty obvious Sheila wasn't coming back. Still, I never felt safe again walking past those bushes. I just couldn't shake the feeling there was something back there, something I feared but should never talk about, waiting.

2

Athlete

"Sissy." The word had now bored its way inside my head. It had carved out a space between my ears where it would echo every time my speech, my gestures, my play, my tears crept out of bounds. I hated this word. I wanted it gone. So I spent the rest of elementary school trying to replace it with another word from that ultimate test of American manhood, sports.

~

"Quarterback."

"Running back."

"Defensive end."

It was the beginning of second grade, and my class was lined up outside our room on a still-temperate early fall morning. Scott Kemper, Markus Banks, and Doug Kellerman were wearing their Pop Warner jerseys, waving around forms for some football-themed fundraiser and tossing out terms that were completely unfamiliar to me. I wanted desperately to join in this guy talk, *be* one of the masculine-sounding things they were naming, even if I had no idea what they were. But the football bus had long since left without me.

When they passed out the information flyers for Pop Warner the previous spring, I stood up very publicly with just about all the other boys to take one. I even brought the form home and tried to discuss it with Yosh one morning before school.

"Yeah! You should go out for *football!*" he bellowed at the kitchen table. It must have been a relief to see his seventh kid, who was starting to seem a little funny, show an interest in sports. But that was about all he had to contribute to the conversation. He didn't know a thing about the game.

When it came to being a sports parent, Yosh's score was basically zero. I can't think of a single time I threw him anything in our backyard but a can of beer. He never watched football, baseball, or basketball on TV, nor did he ever spend Saturdays tossing a Wiffle Ball to his boys, like the dads I saw on television. Instead, he was tossing back shots at Club Royale or the VFW hall, with his other boys.

To be fair, though, I can't lay my poor preparation or lack of motivation for Pop Warner solely at Yosh's feet. Up to this point, my entire body of knowledge about football came from having watched five minutes of a Sunday afternoon game in which one team (the Green Bay Packers?) turned it around against another team (the Dallas Cowboys?) with a Hail Mary play just as the clock ran out. It all felt thrilling for a few minutes, and after the game I ran into my bedroom and jumped on and off my bed, pantomiming long passes and catches that simulated the game-ending touchdown. But I must have picked up one other thing watching that Sunday afternoon Packers-Cowboys game: that football was a rough and dirty world where I'd never fit in. Before I even noticed, the Pop Warner deadline came and went, and I never mentioned it again.

The next spring, I came up with a new strategy to de-sissify myself. I went back to Yosh with another form and got another booming response from the breakfast table.

"Yeah! You should go out for *baseball!*"

I handed him the Little League application, which listed the pay-to-play fee, and asked if he'd write a check.

First, he deflected my question: "I don't know where the checks are. Ask Mommy." Then, he returned to his sports dad impersonation: "So—what position are you gonna try out for?"

I had no idea how to answer this question. There were very few positions I'd even heard of. I knew there was a first baseman, a second baseman, and a third baseman, but I had no way of explaining why I wanted to be one over the other. So I just named the only other position I knew.

"I don't know. I was thinking about trying out for pitcher."

"Oh, you're one with the arm! I thought so!"

Another kid with another father might have felt encouraged by this response, inspired by this vote of confidence to make his dad proud, but it just made me suspicious. I thought, if my father thinks I have a good pitching arm—a notion he has no evidence to support—maybe this whole thing is baloney. But he was kind of supporting me, so I followed through and went to my mother with the application form.

"Baseball? You don't know how to play baseball!" Sophie decreed, obviously annoyed that I was even asking given my lack of interest and participation in sports up to this point.

I should have known better. While Yosh had pretty much continued on his merry, liquored-up way after Thomas's birth two years before, Sophie had sunk more deeply into the role of harried wife and mother, now with eight children to feed and clothe. Her once deep-brown hair graying fast, her face getting thinner, and her heart growing increasingly bitter at forty-five, by this point my mother seemed to have less and less that gave her joy: maybe the blond two-year-old she rocked to sleep on her lap while watching the afternoon soap operas, but certainly not the increasingly effeminate second-grader who now, ridiculously, wanted to join Little League.

"How would you even get there? Who's gonna take you?" asked Sophie rhetorically, to remind me that she didn't have a driver's license.

"Daddy?" I offered as a counter, though now I realized she had checkmate.

I had heard all the stories: my older siblings stranded in remote parts of town or in neighboring towns—waiting out in the cold in front of the YMCA or the pizzeria—while Yosh, who was supposed to have picked them up, lost all track of time at a beer joint. So the deadline for Little League also came and went.

I thought for a few days about asking my parents if I could join Boy Scouts. It wasn't really a sport, but I wouldn't sink an entire team if I screwed up, and at least it had the word "boy" in it. But after the baseball debacle, my brother Benny told me that the real reason Sophie said no to Little League was that we couldn't afford the fee. I didn't know if this was true or not, but Boy Scouts had a fee, too—and meetings where I would need to be dropped off and picked up—so I didn't bother to ask. I knew I was going to have to solve this problem on my own.

~

During the summers I was in elementary school, the local parks department ran an activities program at each of seven or eight parks around town, a sort of public day camp for kids whose parents couldn't afford the real thing. Our closest park was only three blocks from our house, on Clark Avenue, and was unimaginatively named Clark Avenue Park. It wasn't one of the better ones—it didn't have a pool or anything. It was just a dirt and grass field of swings, monkey bars, and picnic tables, bounded by an unpainted split-rail fence. But there were two ongoing tournaments you could take part in that vaguely approximated the experience of a competitive sport.

First, there was tetherball, but after three or four games I learned to avoid this humiliation before it could become Clark Avenue legend. I could never punch the ball hard enough, and I'd end up getting pinned to the pole, wrapped inside like a mummy propped up in a museum display. So by process of elimination, Nok Hockey—a precursor to electric air hockey with a wooden board and puck—became my "sport" of choice.

Despite my complete lack of athleticism, I was a passable Nok Hockey player. I could win an occasional game and maybe even enjoy a string of three or four victories before somebody picked me off. That is, unless Debbie MacNamara was around. Debbie was the undisputed, unstoppable champion of Nok Hockey at Clark Avenue. When she reached the winning score of eleven points—which she often did in less than a minute—she would dust off her hands and, with a twinkly smile, call out, "Game. Next victim!"

Debbie was blonde, freckled, and tomboyishly cute, and her dominance of the game was so complete you couldn't blame her for flaunting it a little. Besides, I was more interested in her friend and frequent sidekick at the Nok Hockey table, Gina Rosario. Much more typically feminine than Debbie, Gina never stooped to playing Nok Hockey—she seemed content to watch Debbie humiliate one boy after another while brushing her long brown hair.

"Aren't you gonna play?" Gina asked me one day while I contemplated the wisdom of challenging Debbie to a game.

"I don't know. Debbie always beats me."

"She beats everybody," said Gina, with a roll of her dark brown eyes. "Don't worry about it."

"Yeah," I shrugged.

"Don't you have a brother? That red-haired kid? I haven't seen him here lately."

As I fell into Gina's dark eyes, I started to forget myself, and my end of the conversation devolved into a meandering babble: "My brother, Benny? Yeah, he used to come here and play Nok Hockey, too, but now he's going into fifth grade, so he's too *mature*. He just turned ten, and he thinks that makes him a teenager already. He walks around the house . . ."

As I chattered on, I realized I was talking with my hands and letting my voice go up to the register that sometimes resulted in my getting those funny looks and snickers at school. But Gina seemed interested in it all, and it felt good just to be myself for a few minutes.

"You're funny," she chuckled, and it suddenly dawned on me: *Does Gina Rosario like me? Like,* like *me? She's really pretty and almost a fourth-grader, so having her as my girlfriend could earn me some major guy points.*

Starting to feel like a bit of a ladies' man, I flirted back. "I'm funny? What do you mean?"

I saw Gina try to puzzle out what she was thinking, scrunching up her face as if trying to solve a hard math problem. Then she finally came out with it: "I don't know. You're sort of—girlish."

Girlish?

Too shell-shocked to challenge Gina on her assessment of me—and what was there to challenge?—I said I "just remembered something" and needed to go home. If Gina had any reaction to my sudden change in demeanor, I didn't notice or care. While Debbie continued her decimation of the boys playing the game, I left Gina midconversation and walked away, my gaze dead ahead. With silent tears filling my eyes, I trudged toward the bike rack, unlocked my red, banana-seat Murray, and rode away.

Passing the tall hedgerow that led up to the intersection of Cleveland Street and Union Avenue, a blind corner where I'd been knocked off my bicycle by a moving car once before, it didn't occur to me to look or even care if any cars were coming. All I could think about was the new word now banging around inside my head, in the space where "sissy" had taken up residence a couple of years before. It spun out into a spiral of questions: Is this *bike* girlish? Are my *clothes* girlish? Do I *look* girlish?

Talk girlish? *Walk* girlish? *Act* girlish? Does *Debbie* think I'm girlish, too? Have other kids at the park been talking all summer about how *girlish* I am?

I didn't know the answers to any of these questions. All I knew was that Gina Rosario had confirmed something Sheila Feldman had put her finger on two years earlier. I'd tried to control it. I'd checked the register of my voice, toned down my gestures, zipped my lip a million times when I was dying to go on and on about *The Brady Bunch*, but obviously none of it was enough. So I just avoided Clark Avenue for the rest of the summer.

~

With the football field, the baseball field, and now the Nok Hockey table all off-limits, I put my sports dreams on hold for a while and spent the rest of that summer on our living room sofa. Day after sunny day, I watched game shows on the twenty-five-inch GE console that played constantly in the corner of the room.

Planted on the beige and brown geometric upholstery all morning and into the afternoon, I watched classics like *Jeopardy!* and *Password* and more obscure shows nobody remembers anymore like *Three on a Match* and *The Who, What, or Where Game*. While the other boys in the neighborhood were worshiping the star players on the Yankees and the Mets, whose names I could never remember, my idols were Bob Barker, Wink Martindale, and a young, handsome Alex Trebek.

Game shows came into our living room from a far-off place, a safe, precious corner of the world where people were rewarded for the things *I* was good at: answering questions, solving puzzles, guessing the value of a prize. You didn't have to run the fastest, throw anything the farthest, or land a puck in a goal. At least in those days, everybody on game shows was nice to one another. Even the losers were treated with dignity and given "lovely parting gifts" to take home. And there were good-looking, sharply dressed hosts with charm, wit, and pearly white smiles. Bob Barker was the funny one, always joking around and making everyone laugh and feel comfortable. Bill Cullen was the kindly older gentleman, reassuring contestants who were doing poorly that it was still "anybody's game." And *Jackpot*'s Geoff Edwards was the dreamy one. In contrast to the more buttoned-up hosts, the boyishly attractive Edwards wore a leisure suit without a tie, leaving his shirt unbuttoned just enough to interest me in a way I didn't quite understand. Maybe *that's* what I could become when I grow up, I thought, wondering what college you could go to and become a really good game show host.

Sophie's reaction to my new obsession was mostly one of perplexed resignation. On the one hand, she couldn't understand why I wasn't going to the park anymore. On the other hand, she was starting to expect unexpected behaviors from me. Occasionally, she'd set down her laundry basket or her can of off-brand Lemon Pledge for a few minutes and step into my question-and-answer world. A typical morning in front of the game shows would pass something like this:

"What European capital is known as the city of lights?" asks host Jack Narz.

"Rome, third row!" Sophie says, as she rounds the corner into the living room and dumps an armful of clothes onto the opposite side of the couch from where I'm sitting. We're watching *Now You See It*, in which the answers to trivia questions are buried in a sea of letters, like in the word search puzzles you see elderly people doing on airplanes.

Slouching under the weight of her morning chores, my mother stands still for a few seconds, her eyes fixed to the screen while she waits for confirmation. I know it's Paris in the second row, but I don't say anything and allow her to think, at least for a few seconds, she's figured out the answer before the contestants on TV have.

"Paris, second row, third position." says a woman on television.

"That's right for five points!" says Jack.

"I don't know," says Sophie (who has been to neither Paris nor Rome). Then she leaves the room to get the next load of towels in the dryer or clean up whatever mess one of us kids has left in the bathroom. I think I care more than she does that she guessed the wrong answer out loud. And while I'll miss having somebody to play the game with, at least I can let the answers rip without worrying I might make my mother feel dumb.

After a few weeks, even the 10 a.m. to 2 p.m. lineup on channels 2, 4, and 7 wasn't enough to satisfy my game show hunger. So when all the morning and early afternoon shows were over I'd go into my room, and the questions and answers would continue, this time with me as master of ceremonies. *Fill the Bill, Bingo for Dollars, Triple Jeopardy*: these were among the shows I invented and hosted after the real ones were over. Each had its own elaborate set of rules. On *Triple Jeopardy*, a spinoff on the original, you earned three times the money for answering any question correctly that your two opponents had gotten wrong (or double the money after one had missed it). The contestants were characters I drew out in crayon, all sitting at podiums, waiting to answer the next question and win fabulous prizes. While my mother transitioned to the late afternoon soap operas—or, as she called them, her "stories"—I gave away large amounts of cash, kitchen appliances, trips to Hawaii, and new cars, all behind the locked door of my bedroom.

"What are you *doing*? What do you *do* in here all day, for Christ's sake?"

Sophie finally confronted me one afternoon as I opened the bedroom door following a tight match on one of my imaginary shows. From the way she asked the question, I could tell she'd been listening—and that it wasn't the first time she'd wanted to know.

"Nothing, just—just homework."

"I don't know," Sophie said with a sigh. She was visibly on edge. "Why don't you—go play outside or go to the park or something. You used to go to the park every day. Now you just sit in here all afternoon making queery papers."

My mother might as well have caught me naked, or trying to clean the sheets from having wet the bed, or worse. She never said another word about it, but the smoldering look in her eyes had said enough.

The echo chamber inside me picked up right where she'd left off, the source of its newest reverberation now my own mother. I didn't even know what the word "queer" meant, only that it was something boys weren't supposed to be, something of which I should feel ashamed. So while Sophie headed to the kitchen to start making dinner, an activity I might have offered to help with under normal circumstances, I stayed in my room and did what I knew I had to do. I immediately canceled all the game shows I'd hosted and, with a cold heart, killed off Bill, Marge, and the other contestants who played them in one swift raid. I tore them all into unrecognizable pieces and threw them in the trash.

~

After the "girlish" incident at Clark Avenue, I must have been the subject of gossip at the MacNamara house, because when school started again Billy MacNamara, Nok Hockey champ Debbie's younger brother, decided he wanted to kill me, or at least inflict serious bodily injury. Almost every day, Billy would sneak up behind me on my walk home from school, buzzing in my ear like the fly you can never get rid of.

"I'm gonna fight you. I'm gonna beat you up!"

And every day, I pretended I didn't hear him while I thought more and more about taking him on. Fighting wasn't a sport, but in some ways it was better. It involved competition, physical prowess, anger, violence—all the things that, by third grade, I was figuring out made you a man.

Billy was freckled and all-American-looking like his sister, and because he was a year younger and a few inches shorter than me, I thought I might have a chance. Plus, just about every other boy I knew at school had been in a fight, and the fact that I hadn't only seemed to validate the things I was now hearing other boys whisper about me, especially during gym class.

"What a queer," Frank Prince would mutter, just loudly enough for me to hear while I ran squealing from the large, gleaming orange projectile during a game of dodge ball.

Or I'd hear "homo, homo . . ." peppering Scott Kemper's conversation after I tripped, thus sinking our team's hope of winning the day's relay race. "He's such a homo."

One day I was walking home for lunch, figuring I'd just eat SpaghettiOs and watch game shows as usual, and Billy came up behind me and performed his daily ritual.

"I'm gonna beat you up!"

"Oh, yeah? I'll beat *you* up. Let's *fight!*" I answered back, in a tough-guy tone that surprised me as much as it did Billy. "When do you wanna *fight?*"

My plan was to make an appointment for the fight to take place some day after school. Besides the fact that I wouldn't have to miss *Jeopardy!*, this would give other kids time to hear about it. I knew that fights drew crowds, and if ours was a big, well-advertised battle of the boys, I could rewrite my entire history in one day. But apparently, in the real world of fighting, it doesn't work this way.

"Right now! I'll fight you right now!" said Billy, eyes bulging, already thirsting for blood.

His wanting to go at it immediately sent me into a panic, but backing down wasn't an option. The fact that we were walking along a sidewalk with a two-lane highway on one side and a stockade fence on the other bought me a little time. But once we turned the corner, and there were houses with front lawns all around, any of which could serve as a fine venue for a fight, it was on. There was no turning back.

We took our stances: Billy's authentic and mean—obviously this wasn't his first fight—mine tentative and stagey, borrowed from all the fights I'd witnessed at school. As Billy came at me and I was about to throw my first punch—or whatever I would have thrown—I suddenly thought of my teacher, Mrs. Tuckerman. How disappointed she would be if she knew I was about to get into a fight.

"You? Fighting? But Michael, you're such a nice boy!" she said in my head, with a sad tone of disapproval that crushed me.

But a second later, Billy approached, and I came to my senses. This wasn't about Mrs. Tuckerman. It was about me and Billy and fists and blood and becoming a boy once and for all.

My memory of the next few seconds is a blur. Did Billy punch me? Did I punch Billy? I only remember that before things could get too serious, a man I often saw waiting at the corner bus stop strode swiftly into the yard we'd chosen for the fight.

"Hey! Break it up! Break it up, you two, right now, or I'm gonna call the police!"

The police?

Billy and I looked at each other, on the same team for half a second, and stopped our swinging for fear of a run-in with the cops. Then, along with the fear, I suddenly felt a rush of something else course through my body: *That "break it up" was for me!* I was a *boy*, in a *fight*, that needed to be *broken up*. Wow.

The man didn't physically separate us. He didn't have to, because it was pretty clear he meant business. Billy's and my eyes met, and with a brief, complicit look, we dispersed toward our respective houses.

Back at school, nothing much changed after my fight with Billy. As a second-grader, Billy was pretty much a social nonentity among my peers, and nobody seemed to talk or even know about what had happened between the two of us. Only one thing was different: Billy MacNamara never bothered me again.

~

The following spring, all of us in Mrs. Tuckerman's class started having impromptu foot races before school on the slope that led up to our classroom door. Maybe it was a hormone surge after my fight with Billy, maybe it was radiation from all the TV I was watching, or maybe I was just growing up, but something caused a growth spurt that made me one of the tallest kids in my class. And every so often, thanks to my longer legs, something unprecedented happened: I won an athletic competition.

On one of the last days of school, Eric Ackerly, the fastest kid in our class and a ringleader in organizing the foot races, made a surprise announcement.

"Now we're gonna have a championship—the three fastest!"

A buzz circulated among the third-graders. I knew Eric meant himself and David McAvoy—that much was without question. But who did Eric think should get the third spot? Then, as if it were obvious, he said, "Me, McAvoy, and Sadowski."

Even with a few victories under my belt, I was flabbergasted to be named for this invitational race—but I couldn't let it show. So with adrenaline pulsing from the bottom of my third-fastest feet to the crown of my now-swelling head, I lined up, all stone-faced intensity, next to Eric and David, as if it just came naturally.

"On your mark! Get set! Go!"

Flying down the hill, I pictured the upset I was going to pull off on my two shorter classmates while the others cheered, applauded, and shouted my name. At the end of the downhill stretch I was in third place, but I thought I could make up lost ground with longer strides on the uphill sprint. I pushed and pushed up the hill and moved closer and closer to Eric and David.

Then, mere seconds after the race began, it was over, turning out exactly as the odds-makers would have predicted: Eric first, David second, me third. Mrs. Tuckerman opened the door and I walked through it, one among twenty-two or so third-graders, and another ordinary school day began. It was hard not to feel deflated—I could have won so much more than a race in those thirty seconds before school. But I also felt like everyone was looking at me a little differently, or maybe it was that they're *weren't* looking at me differently. That morning, I wasn't a sissy, or girlish, or queer, or a homo. For one brief, precious moment, I was just one of the guys.

~

In fourth grade, I tried desperately to revive the early-morning races. My legs had grown even longer over the summer, so I thought I had a shot not only at winning a race or two but maybe even being the best. I lobbied, cajoled, tried to appeal to my classmates' sense of nostalgia for that glorious third-grade spring.

"Remember those races we used to have before school? That was so much fun!"

But no one seemed interested. I had trouble drumming up participation in a morning pastime from which all of my peers, even Eric Ackerly, had moved on. I would have to wait until fifth grade, the last year of elementary school, for my shot at athletic glory.

Field Day was the biggest event of the year at Van Derveer Elementary, an Olympics-like tournament in which every fifth-grade class competed to determine which would be crowned the best. Here, at last, I would parlay my past success as a sprinter into a final, blazing victory. I'd show everybody, especially the boys who'd rolled their eyes at me and muttered "homo" when I screwed up in gym class, that I'd become the fastest kid in school. I'd leave them all in a cloud of bewildered, awe-struck dust.

Preparations for Field Day began with qualifying heats led by Mrs. Finch, our gym teacher, in the early spring. As the qualifier for each big race—the fifty-yard dash, the hundred-yard dash—approached, I told myself it would be *my* event, the one that tapped into my specific strengths as a runner. But after enough of these trials, I learned that a lot of kids had caught up to me height-wise—and, more importantly, speed-wise—in the last two years. I didn't qualify for any of the big races. My fantasy of breaking the tape to the cheers of my classmates was not to be, and I was relegated to the broad jump, probably the biggest "who cares?" competition of the day. Everybody knew that the kids assigned to the broad jump weren't really the best jumpers; they were just the ones Mrs. Finch didn't know what else to do with.

As Field Day approached, Mrs. Finch tried to drum up excitement like a sixty-year-old cheerleader who didn't know any good cheers: "Two, four, six, eight! Who do we appreciate? Fifth-graders!"

Overly tanned, leather-skinned, and always smelling of the last cigarette she'd smoked, I didn't like Mrs. Finch, and my lousy team placement on the broad jump did little to improve my opinion of her. So maybe it was passive aggressiveness or maybe it was just preteen for-getfulness, but when the sunny June Friday momentously marked on the school calendar as Field Day finally arrived, I made a colossal error. Instead of the sneakers that were required every day we had gym, let alone at a special event like Field Day, I wore brown, hard-soled leather shoes to school. And because we weren't allowed to go home for lunch that day—we would eat in our classrooms and then head to the play-ground right afterward—I couldn't go home and change. The best I could hope for was that nobody would look down at my feet all day.

"You don't have sneakers on!" whispered Rudy Francino within the first five minutes of school, moon-faced, as if it were the biggest scandal ever to have hit Van Derveer. "Mrs. Finch is gonna yell at you! She might not even let you do Field Day!"

"Yes, she will," I assured Rudy, while I panicked that here it was, not even 9 a.m., and somebody had already noticed my shoes. "I'm in the broad jump. I can jump even farther in these. You'll see."

After lunch, we filed down to the playground and gathered with all the other fifth-grade classes. Mrs. Finch ordered us to line up by class so that she could walk back and forth, clipboard in hand, and inspect the troops. Strategically, I positioned my feet behind those of Brad Rosenthal—who spent thirteen years next to me in alphabetical order—hoping that my recently shined, lace-up Oxfords could escape Mrs. Finch's gaze. When she got to our end of the line, she looked straight down and stopped dead in her tracks.

"Michael, *where* are your sneakers?"

"I'm doing the broad jump, so—I—thought I could wear shoes today."

"No, you may not! Now you just step right over there." She was point-ing to an area in the middle of the playground, far from where the whole rest of the fifth grade was standing. "You cannot participate in Field Day if you're not wearing sneakers!"

Not looking at any of the other kids, I stepped out of the line and clip-clopped toward the region of social Siberia where Mrs. Finch had ordered me to go. After a minute or two getting everyone dispatched for warm-ups, she left the group to come and deal with me.

"Now, *why* don't you have your sneakers?" she asked, in a sigh that reminded me a little bit of my mother's.

"I don't know," I mumbled, staring at the ground. "I just forgot them."

At a temporary loss for words, Mrs. Finch just looked at the sky. Then, as if it came to her in a revelation from above, she found the perfect parting shot.

"You forgot your *sneakers*? On *Field Day*?" she brayed, staring me right in the eyes. And then, with a low, slow sneer of disgust, she said, "What *are* you, some kind of a *sissy*? You *must* be!"

Mrs. Finch let her eyes and her words bore into me for a few more endless-seeming seconds. Then, finally done with me, she did a 180 on her Keds and turned away. She marched back to kick off the festivities and left me, the Field Day exile, in the middle of the playground.

As I watched her go, I stood stunned for a minute or two. Then I walked over to a high metal stool someone had left alongside the building. I sat down and felt the weight of my heavy leather shoes pulling down on my feet, which didn't quite touch the ground.

Soon I heard the faint screech of Mrs. Finch's whistle from the other side of the playground. Field Day was starting not fifty yards away, on the grassy field across the asphalt from where I sat. But the longer I sat there, the more it all just receded into the distance—the sprints, the broad jump, the kids now part of a world from which I felt completely separate. I was deep inside myself now, Mrs. Finch's words booming over and over in a now-familiar echo that filled my head, my chest, my entire body. Right around the corner from the row of bushes where Sheila Feldman had branded me a sissy in first grade, Mrs. Finch had issued the final verdict. Five years of elementary school, of efforts to cut that word and everything it meant out from inside me, had come down to this.

At some point—it felt like hours but was probably only about forty-five minutes—the bell rang. Field Day was over. I have no idea who won.

3

The Men in the Mirror

Anyone from a normal-sized family might assume that growing up with a father and three older brothers, I'd have had a wealth of men around the house to help me figure out what a man was supposed to look like, talk like, walk like, be like. As an adult, I see their images all the time in my bathroom mirror, have moments while shaving or combing my hair when one of my brothers' faces—or even my father's face—is staring back at me. Suddenly I'll catch a glimpse of the eyes or the set of the jaw, features that mark us as unmistakable members of the tribe.

Yet as anyone who grew up with a lot of siblings will tell you, large families—especially those with significant age gaps—break into two, sometimes even three smaller families when these gaps run across fifteen or, as in our case, more than twenty years. Each group in its course moves through the pangs of childhood and adolescence, consumes the bulk of their parents' attention and financial resources, then grows up and leaves the house just in time for the next group to take over their bedrooms.

Most of my childhood memories of my eldest brother, George, involve his comings and goings. George was a light-haired, bespectacled science wiz who avoided a geek persona with good looks, an obsession with the Yankees, and a steady hometown girlfriend who, years later, became his wife. He was the first person in our family to attend college, a source of great pride for Sophie and the subject of much bragging from Yosh, who told anyone who would listen that his son attended the University of Maryland.

Whenever George was coming home on a school break, my head buzzed in anticipation. Even though it meant there would be not just nine but ten people vying for the one overworked bathroom in our tiny Cape Cod, his arrival always broke the monotony of daily life in the way every child cherishes. Sophie would stock the shelves with George's favorite treats, Drake's Devil Dogs and Tastykake Krimpets, which when he was around the rest of us weren't allowed to touch. I'd overhear stories about his classes and his dorm and the antiwar protests that were happening on campus, tales from a world I could barely imagine. Yet with each visit, George seemed a bit more like a stranger. The gulf between him and us, especially between him and my father, grew wider with every class he took, every professor or preppy he met in College Park.

"Oh, you're the big college man now!" high school dropout Yosh would profess with artificial disdain whenever George had the temerity to express an opinion. Or, if George said something Yosh didn't understand at all, my father would just dismiss it as "college shit" and leave the room.

The fall I started second grade, George moved straight from undergrad into a doctoral program at MIT. Yes, the first offspring of Yosh and Sophie, who never went past tenth and twelfth grades respectively, earned a full ride at one of the world's leading technological institutions after a spectacular undergraduate run in Maryland. While in grad school, George married his hometown girlfriend, Liz, and then they moved to western Pennsylvania for George's first post-MIT job. Except for a few shorts visits two or three times a year, I never saw him on Lincoln Avenue again.

~

If George was the academic superstar, Larry, four years younger, was the lovable troublemaker. Broken windows in the neighborhood, detention for pulling a girl's ponytail—as a boy, Larry would come home and sheepishly report incidents like these to my mother, who would throw up her hands and ask the picture of Jesus in our kitchen how her first two sons could possibly have been born so different. Yet Larry's path into my mother's heart was paved with the very shenanigans that grayed her hair—and cost her a fair amount of money. Even after Larry drove my mother toward Yosh's liquor cabinet a time or two, all was soon forgiven because he was the one who could make everybody laugh.

Larry attended community college and lived at home during most of my elementary school years, but I hardly ever saw him, his time occupied with his classes, his girlfriend, his souped-up Pontiac GTO, and two hobbies that came to define him to me.

Weekday mornings while getting ready for school, I would routinely start the day with a trip to the basement to pee in the pit of our sump pump. (Large families with only one bathroom come up with many creative solutions to the morning routine.) Descending the stairs, sometimes I would detect a foul, fishy smell and then spy a half-dozen or so glassy eyes staring up at me from atop my mother's chest freezer. They would dare me to touch their shiny silver scales, even pick them up as I had seen men do posing for photographs, showing off the big catch of the day. I wanted to want to touch them. I wanted to want to go out by the lake like Larry did, put a slimy worm on a hook, jerk back the pole, and pull up a catch, its mouth bloody while it gasped for breath and wriggled to get away. But obviously something was wrong with me, because I wanted nothing to do with touching, catching, hooking, cooking, or eating these revolting, helpless creatures.

On Saturday mornings, the basement discoveries of Larry's leave-behinds were often of a different sort. During commercial breaks in my TV lineup of *Sabrina, the Teenage Witch, Scooby-Doo,* and *Josie and the Pussycats,* my path to the basement sump pump would suddenly be blocked by a deer carcass twice my size hanging from the ceiling, its red, sinewy guts still smelling of the fresh blood and fur it would no longer need. The first few times I made these grisly discoveries, I stared at them for a long time, tried to feel something other than disgust and pity, connect to a thirst for blood and shooting and death that men were apparently supposed to have. Eventually, the deer would be transformed into creepy mounted heads with marbles for eyes (one of which Larry had nailed into the wood paneling of his bedroom) and cuts of meat wrapped up in the basement chest freezer that, when my mother served it, I refused to eat. How could I eat Bambi's mother after she'd gazed at me with her defenseless, trusting eyes?

To me, hunting and fishing were about killing things that had done nothing to harm you. (I didn't yet see the connection to the fried chicken, fish sticks, and hamburgers I gladly ate for dinner most nights.) It didn't make any sense. Larry was the one in our family who was always smiling, telling jokes, trying to lighten the mood and make people feel good. I couldn't fathom why he would choose to kill and gut these animals. And I never even tried to understand it, because I knew I could never do it.

Five days after my twelfth birthday, Larry got married and moved out.

~

BennyandMichael can stay home with your father.

BennyandMichael, take out the garbage!

Goddammit! Look what BennyandMichael did! They had chocolate milk and got Nestlé's Quik all over my clean floor!

Two years and four months older than me, Benny had fiery red hair and a fiery brain. Later in life, he would receive more awards than anyone else at his middle school graduation and be class salutatorian in high school. Since we were the closest in age of any of the boys in our family, Benny and I shared a room and did a lot of things together. We had ongoing tournaments of *Monopoly* (he always won), *Stratego* (he always won), and *The Game of Life* (he usually won, the wheel in the middle occasionally rescuing me despite my inferior career and investment choices). We acted out episodes of *Lost in Space* when our cousins came over. We made mystery dramas on our cassette tape recorder, creating elaborate whodunits complete with red herrings, unfaithful spouses, and surprise reveals that we begged our uninterested older siblings to listen to. ("This one's really good. You won't be able to figure out who did it!") When *The Brady Bunch* became our favorite show, we lobbied successfully for bunk beds so that our bedroom could have the feel of a TV sitcom, even if the rest of our life was nothing like one.

Benny's and my frequent companionship—as well as our proximity to one another in both age and household geography—led the rest of the family, especially my mother, to talk about us in one breath when discussing everything from food preferences to transportation logistics to who left the back door open and let all those bugs in.

"Look at these flies! BennyandMichael were going in and out, in and out all day!" my mother would say, even if one of us hadn't been home for hours.

I hated getting blamed for things I had no part in. But Benny hated it even more because it meant getting lumped in with me, who—in addition to being the kid brother who embarrassed him at school by my very existence—interfered with his own effort to remake his identity.

As several classic family photos documented, Benny had liked to play with dolls as a preschooler, so he had his own sissy reputation to live down. Being forever associated with a younger brother who other people thought was girlish didn't help his cause. So Benny, despite all the things we did together, kept a certain distance from me. And as I wandered through my childhood looking for images of the man I wanted to become, I guess I kept a certain distance, too. Benny and I were just too much alike.

~

Then there were my sisters' boyfriends, who eventually became their fiancés and husbands.

Donna was two years younger than George and two years older than Larry. Although Donna did well in school, being a girl in our family meant that there were no expectations—nor was there any financial support—for you to attend college. So Donna got a job as a bank teller and, at age nineteen, moved out and married Steve, one of her regular customers. An even more avid hunter than Larry, Steve tripled the number of deer carcasses one might find in our basement during hunting season.

Nancy and Kathy were teenagers during my childhood, seven and six years older than me, respectively. Because they were just a year apart and shared a room, they had their own mushed-together family moniker.

"NancyKathy!" my mother would yell up the stairs on a Saturday morning. "I need one of yous to vacuum and one of yous to dust the furniture. Come down here!"

Once Nancy and Kathy started high school, boys started to come into the picture. And when I was in third grade, a new ray of hope arrived in the form of Mark, star running back of the Somerville High School football team.

When Nancy and Mark became a couple, I started going to the games regularly, telling anyone who would listen that my sister's boyfriend was number 23, the player everyone was talking about. Nancy and Mark were both brown-haired and gorgeous performing their respective roles under the Friday night lights—she cheering the team on as a member of the pep club, he thrilling the crowd with runs into the end zone. Not knowing the least bit about the rules of football or what was happening on the field, I paid little attention to the game itself. But I was intoxicated by the trappings of the cool fall evenings at Somerville's Brooks Field: the smell of boiled hot dogs and cocoa at the concession stand; the big electric scoreboard counting down the seconds and tracking every advance; the announcements on the loudspeaker; the crowd riveted at the edge of their bleacher seats.

All this will be mine one day, I would think, while I breathed in the chocolate-scented steam from my styrofoam cup and planned my varsity football career seven years hence. Momentarily forgetting all my abortive attempts at athletic glory, I fantasized that Mark would teach me everything I needed to know in a few easy lessons: how to catch a pass while running into the end zone, where exactly to put my fingers on the laces for maximum distance and spin. Mark was much more attentive to his girlfriend's sissy little brother than any high school football star needed to be, and he probably would have taught me a few of those things if I'd asked. But I couldn't bring myself to do it, because wasn't I supposed to know them already?

~

Finally, there was my father, who spent every fair-weather Sunday of my childhood gazing at the sky. He wasn't a poet or a meteorologist. By profession, he was a factory worker. Monday through Friday, he mixed paint on a 3-to-11 night shift in South Bound Brook, New Jersey, where a cluster of chemical factories gave the air a sickly sweet, medicinal smell the rest of us didn't have to deal with in slightly more upscale Somerville. But on weekends, Yosh was a sky gazer, a sportsman in his own right. He was a pigeon racer.

On Saturday afternoons, my father would take a crate of homing pigeons, maybe a dozen of the most promising from his flock of about sixty, to a place our family simply called "the pigeon club." (It had a long, official name none of us could remember.) Then as dusk started to fall, someone at the club would put all the members' birds in a truck, drive west, and release them somewhere along a highway in Pennsylvania.

The next morning, the vigil began. Armed with a six-pack of Schaefer in one hand and a twelve-foot bamboo pole in the other, Yosh would head for the faux-redwood picnic table in our backyard and sit there for hours, scanning the heavens. Although it never occurred to me at the time, there was probably some connection between my father's military service and his affinity for things that flew. During World War II, Yosh had served in the army as a paratrooper, had flown in helicopters over Belgium and France, then parachuted into active battlefields and once, as one of his favorite stories went, an ice-cold river. As a kid, my father's war tales always bored me or, more often, filled me with shame, the military being yet another world of men where I knew I'd never fit in. But now I wonder if, when he looked up at the clouds from our back- yard waiting for the pigeons to come home, he ever thought about his own time in the sky.

Sometimes my father was joined in his Sunday ritual by his younger brother, my Uncle Ted, who lived next door and was also a member of the pigeon club. But Uncle Ted had a mysterious life in the city, a pos- sible "ladyfriend" my siblings and I speculated wildly about but never met. By the afternoon, Ted would lose interest in the pigeon race. He'd don his Sunday best, finish it off with a splash of Aqua Velva, and hop the bus to meet whoever was waiting for him at Port Authority, leaving Yosh behind in Jersey to finish the waiting game alone.

When one of my father's flock showed up—as long as he hadn't already had too many beers to notice—he would silently rise to his feet and slowly pick up the bamboo pole. Tiptoeing, he would then use the pole to guide the birds, ever so gently, back into the open cages atop a ramshackle outbuilding in our backyard that was the color of Dijon mustard.

Yosh's pigeon coop was, to put it gently, a bit different from what the other families in our suburban neighborhood had in their backyards in the early seventies: above-ground swimming pools, river canoes, metal storage sheds from Sears painted to look like barns or country cottages. And, because we lived on a corner lot, it was impossible for anyone who drove or walked past our house to miss it. Its jarring color aside, it was as wide as a three-car garage, and I suppose because one side of it was a sagging, lean-to carport, we euphemistically referred to it as "the garage" even though no one ever kept a car in it.

The door into the pigeon pens was one I remember walking through only once during my childhood. My father and Uncle Ted were both going to be out all day and, probably having been told "forget it" by my mother and older siblings, Yosh asked me to feed the birds. By now, I'd been called a sissy and a queer enough times that the labels were starting to stick, so I couldn't say I was scared. But I had no idea what would happen when I finally got up the nerve to enter the pigeons' inner sanctum.

Carrying a soup can full of feed in each trembling hand, I was immediately assaulted by gray and white flying rats fluttering and cooing around my face. The thick, unventilated stink of bird poop and filthy feathers coated my nose, my throat, my lungs. Beneath me, I saw the industrial-gray floor almost completely covered with white splotches, which even then I knew could carry disease. I tossed the feed toward the troughs so fast I landed most of it on the floor, which produced another coo and flutter around my face and feet, slammed the door behind me, and vowed never to open it again.

Still, undaunted by my obvious lack of interest in the pigeons, Yosh brought me to the club headquarters one day and tried to get me involved in the goings-on there. Holding court at the fully stocked bar, he introduced me to the other members as his boy—a word that made me cringe given how little like a boy I was starting to feel. And, his green eyes twinkling after his first shot of whiskey, he bragged about my grades, which made me cringe even more.

"Yeah, I call this one the professor. You should see his report card—straight As! He's a real fart smeller, I'm tellin' ya!"

After showing me how to get my own Cokes from the bar tap, Yosh pointed me toward the other kids at the club and encouraged me to "socialize," a way of moving through the world he always recommended in implicit contrast to my misanthropic mother.

"What's wrong with going out, having a drink once in a while?" I'd once heard Yosh ask Sophie when she'd criticized him for hanging out in bars while she was at home taking care of their eight kids. "You gotta socialize with people. That's what's wrong with you. You don't know how to socialize."

"*Socialize?*" she'd answered. "With who? The people at a *beer joint?* Get the hell outta here! No, thanks."

While Yosh disappeared into the crowd to socialize and take advantage of the "free" liquor he paid for with his membership dues, I floundered in the sea of white undershirts and Dickies work pants that was the pigeon club social scene. The only other kids my age I could find to talk to were two brothers with ruddy faces and blond crew cuts whose names I remember as Hykel and Michael—no kidding. Benny and I had played with them once at the pigeon club's annual picnic, so with no other options in sight I said hi. Hykel and Michael were nice enough kids, but they were *real* boys. All they wanted to do was talk about fishing and pick up the slimy worms we found in the dirt near the front door so that they could save them for bait. I had no interest in fishing, and even less in touching worms.

"There's one," I mumbled over and over, pointing out worms and feeling pangs of guilt as Hykel and Michael condemned them to their miserable fate in a Solo cup. Once all the available worms had been collected and were slithering around the cup looking for a way out, I ran out of things to talk to Hykel and Michael about. So I played with the soda jets for a while—I learned what Coke, ginger ale, and 7-Up taste like all mixed together—and waited until Yosh was done socializing so that I could do what I'd wanted to do since the moment we'd arrived: go home and watch TV.

In all the years I can remember, Yosh never won a pigeon race. In an earlier era, he and Uncle Ted had obviously had their glory days, as the "Sadowski Bros." trophies Uncle Ted proudly displayed on a shelf in his house proved. But the older Yosh of my childhood never came home with a trophy or cash prize. Instead of ending with a victory celebration and pizza for the whole family, Sunday morning pigeon racing always deteriorated into Sunday afternoon beer drinking: the Schaefer cans stacked up in a pyramid on the picnic table, Yosh out cold on the seat, his bamboo pole resting on the ground doing absolutely nothing, and the pigeons coming home whenever they damn well pleased.

At some point—I'm not sure when—Yosh set down his bamboo pole for good. I don't remember his making any firm decision to stop racing. In my memory, it all just fades away. But the pigeon coop remained standing, birdless, for many years after my parents' house was packed up and sold. Then one day, decades after the last Sadowski Bros. race had been run, a woman lost control of her car on the two-lane highway that ran behind our old house. She drove clear across the back neighbors' yard and barreled into the coop, knocking most of it to the ground. Uncle Ted, who still lived in the house next door, wept at the destruction of this last vestige of a life gone by. Then he used the insurance money to put up a store-bought lawnmower shed, painted in cheery colors to look like a country cottage.

4

My Mother's Savior

In the dark, catastrophe seems possible, sometimes even certain.

In a memory that blends many similar nights into one, I'm ten years old. It's midnight, and I'm lying in the upper bunk of Benny's and my Brady Bunch beds, staring at the ceiling less than two feet above my head. Familiar shouts of goddammit, sonofabitch, and shit reverberate through the walls, then trail off into unintelligible specifics. Then more expletives ring out, followed by banging and crashing sounds—bodies shoved against walls that creak with the pressure, a lamp falling off a table, a heavy cut-glass ashtray hitting the floor.

Neither Benny nor I say anything about the sounds penetrating the two thin layers of sheetrock that separate my parents' bedroom from ours. Maybe Benny lets out a sigh as if to say, "I'm trying to get some sleep," but neither of us speaks to the churning in our guts, the tension between our parents that's now reverberating in our own bodies, the terror that something awful and irrevocable is about to happen. I wonder what Nancy and Kathy can hear upstairs, but I know I'll never ask them. Maybe they don't hear anything. Maybe Benny doesn't hear anything either. Maybe I'm the only one lying here, overdramatizing things, imagining our world is coming to an end.

Maybe this has something to do with why, to this day, I can rarely sleep through the night.

~

My all-time favorite picture in our family photo box, one I always looked for in the random shuffle of Kodak and Polaroid snapshots until it strangely went missing one day, was taken at my parents' twenty-fifth anniversary party, just before I turned nine. In the photograph as I recall it, Sophie wears a brown, crew-neck polyester pant suit, Yosh a pair of blue-green work chinos and a tan button-down shirt undone one button too many, a telltale sign of the one beer too many he's already downed even though it's still the middle of the afternoon. Sophie looks up at the camera with a "can't live with him, can't live without him" smirk while she feeds Yosh the first slice of a white sheet cake, decorated with the words "happy anniversary" in thinly piped blue frosting. My parents' quarter century as a couple summed up in a four-by-six print: their courtship, in an era when people still used that word; Sophie anxiously awaiting Yosh's return from the war; the big church wedding, followed by the honeymoon at Niagara Falls; the birth of their first child—then their second, then their third, then all the rest; Sophie's dollar-stretching to make ends meet on Yosh's factory-worker salary; the building and setting up of the house on the tiny lot my grandmother had given them; the shared pride at watching George go off and be the first one in our family to attend college.

By day, I clung to this image of my parents as a smiling middle-aged pair—a zany couple right out of a sitcom ad in the *TV Guide*—even as by night I listened to the shouting and swearing and shoving. During their late-night battles, it was always my mother's safety, never my father's, I panicked about as I lay in bed, vividly imagining the worst but otherwise doing nothing.

Is Mommy unconscious? Did she have a heart attack? Or did she hit the back of her head on the corner of their nightstand and die instantly, just like that woman on General Hospital?

I didn't think either of my parents really wanted to kill the other, but I knew that when Yosh was drunk, he lost control over his body, so anything was possible. And Sophie, whatever she thought about my "queery papers" or about me, was still my mother. She was a part of my everyday life in a way that Yosh wasn't. Even when he worked days, my father was rarely home from Club Royale or whatever beer joint he'd stopped at after work in time for dinner. Weeknight table talk where Dad gave advice while Mom nodded in agreement happened only on the family comedies I cherished—both contemporary ones like *The Brady Bunch* and the old reruns I watched in my pajamas before school, shows like

Father Knows Best and *Leave It to Beaver*, which depicted family life in broad-stroked, black-and-white bliss.

My mother wasn't exactly Mrs. Brady or Mrs. Cleaver either. When I came home from school, instead of smiling with bemused delight at whatever boyish fix I'd gotten into that day, she'd sigh with frustration at whatever kitchen activity, like shaking the Shake-and-Bake chicken bag, I wanted to join her in that afternoon. But she combed my hair every morning, squeezing my cheeks hard as she tried to get the part just right and mat down the cowlick that stands up in the back of my head to this day. She heated up my SpaghettiOs to just the right temperature when I came home for lunch, and she was always reliably there sorting laundry in the living room when I rushed back at 3:30 to watch our favorite of all the soap operas, *One Life to Live*.

By fourth or fifth grade, my daytime viewing obsession had expanded beyond game shows to the dramas that followed them, a development that did nothing to shore up my attempts to seem like a normal boy.

"Viki knows that Joe's alive?" I'd gasp. "What's she gonna do? Is she gonna leave Steve and go with him?"

"I don't know," Sophie would answer with a sigh, simultaneously glad to have someone to talk to about the latest juicy plot twist and disturbed that it's her ten-year-old son. "She's got a situation alright."

If my mother and I talked at all when I came home from school, it was about Viki's problems, or Nicole's on *The Edge of Night*, or those of one of the other daytime heroines I'd grown to love like surrogate mothers, women who exuded grace and beauty under the direst of circumstances. I could imagine finding a sympathetic ear in one of these women if I described my run-ins with people like Mrs. Finch or shared my midnight anxieties about my parents' violent arguments. Sometimes I fantasized about disclosing to Viki or Nicole my fears of how our family would disintegrate in the wake of an ugly divorce or, worse, how one night I might find my mother lying in a pool of blood on the floor. Those kinds of things happened all the time in their fictional towns. It didn't seem like much of a stretch to imagine it could happen at our house, too.

~

The only memories I have of seeing, as opposed to just hearing, my father during my later elementary school years take place on weekends.

On a quiet Saturday evening when we were already in our pajamas, ready to settle in for a night of *All in the Family*, *Mary Tyler Moore*, and *The Carol Burnett Show*, Yosh would suddenly swing open the back metal storm door after a few hours at the pigeon club or a beer joint.

"Yous look like a buncha girls!" he'd proclaim upon getting his first good look at Benny, Thomas, and me for the week. "That's it! Yous are gonna get haircuts!"

This out-of-the-blue announcement of haircut night would send the three of us scrambling to all hidden corners of the house while Yosh went searching for his Wahl amateur barber kit. I didn't think my hair looked any longer than that of Greg Brady or Keith Partridge, the cool teenagers on TV I wanted to be, but Yosh's charge still stung. In retrospect, I don't think our looking like girls was really what stuck in Yosh's craw—saying that was just his way of getting us to cooperate. To him, long hair was the ultimate sign of youth degeneracy. It conjured images in his mind of hippies, of war protesters who had no gratitude for the sacrifices veterans like him had made for them, of spoiled college kids who were all "on dope."

"Leave 'em alone! Jesus Christ!" Sophie would yell from the next room, her words and tone suggesting she'd put a stop to the whole thing but her fixed position in front of *The Newlywed Game* indicating otherwise. Eventually, my father would nab each of us by the pajama collar from whatever hiding place we'd managed to crouch in and, armed with his haircut weaponry, plunk us into the raised stool he'd placed in the middle of the kitchen. He'd chop out wonky styles that required Sophie to do extensive Monday morning doctoring with Vitalis or Dippity-Do just to make sure we didn't go to school looking like absolute freaks.

If any day around the house was Daddy day, it was Sunday. On Sundays, if there wasn't a pigeon race, Yosh would often occupy my usual spot on the geometric-print sofa and sit all afternoon drinking one Schaefer after another and watching old movies. He loved the black-and-white westerns they showed on Channel 5 and tried to get Benny and me interested in them time after time.

"This is a good one, *Yellow Sky* or somethin', with that there—Peck, what's his name? Siddown and watch it with me. There's gonna be a *showdown*."

In my younger years, I might have enjoyed sitting on the couch with my father, smelling his Old Spice and getting sugared up on the soapy-tasting, violet-scented gum and lozenges he kept in his shirt pocket. But Yosh's movies were filled with images to which I was starting to become highly allergic: cowboys, rifles, dusty pioneer towns that looked nothing like the New Jersey landscape of supermarkets and strip malls I knew and loved. When one of Yosh's westerns was on, I'd flee to our room and play a board game with Benny or, if he didn't want to, with any number of imaginary opponents I could conjure up—anything to avoid having to admit yet again that I wasn't interested in any of the things boys were supposed to like.

Later on Sunday afternoons, if Yosh's movie was over and it wasn't time for supper yet, he would play records on the wood-grained console stereo, which sat on the opposite end of our living room from the wood-grained console TV. Yosh's album collection was made up almost exclusively of male crooners. He had all the big ones like Frank Sinatra and Bing Crosby, but he also had a soft spot for B-listers like Jerry Vale and Vaughn Monroe and bought their records, too. After a few more beers, he'd start to sing along. Yosh could carry a tune well enough, though his droopy eyes and slurred consonants conjured Dean Martin more than the Frank Sinatra he fancied himself to be. Just like his westerns, we kids hated my father's music. We called it farty—as in sung by a bunch of old farts—and couldn't wait until he fell asleep from too many beers so that we could replace it with a Jackson Five album.

If Yosh stayed awake long enough, at some point in the afternoon he'd get to his favorite ballad, a song in waltz time called "Fascination" that Nat King Cole sang gorgeously (though at the time I wrote it off as another one of my father's farty favorites). When Yosh played "Fascination"—or, once he scratched the record beyond usability, sang it a cappella—it was dance time. Cajoling Thomas, then me, then Benny to place our feet on top of his, Yosh would drag us around the living room in a clunky "Papa's Waltz" while he mimicked Nat's buttery baritone:

It was fascination, I know,
And it might have ended right then, at the start.
Just a passing glance, just a brief romance,
And I might have gone on my way, empty-hearted.

It was fascination, I know,
Seeing you alone with the moonlight above,
Then I touch your hand and next moment I kiss you,
Fascination turned to love.

"Fascination" had been Mommy and Daddy's song, he would tell us, as he chopped around his imaginary dance floor, barely able to maintain his own balance let alone that of the five-, ten-, or twelve-year-old boy standing atop his paint-splotched work shoes. Meanwhile Sophie cooked, took a nap, paid bills, did anything else in another room to put distance between herself and the dancing she wanted no part of.

Desperate for confirmation that my parents had once been a normal, loving couple like the ones I saw on TV, I asked my mother if what Daddy said was true, if "Fascination" had really been their song. The first time I asked, Sophie waved off the question with a dismissive gesture and didn't even look up from her checkbook, or the laundry, or whatever she was doing, the top of her graying head my only response. But I really wanted to know, so I kept asking. Finally, she gave me an answer—probably just to get me to stop with the questions already—and said she didn't remember.

~

We were not, in any way, an affectionate family. Even simple pleasantries like "please," "thank you," and "you're welcome" were rare, and "I love you" was utterly, completely outside the family lexicon. I don't remember anyone ever saying those words to anyone, under any circumstances, throughout my childhood. I do remember one instance of my mother responding to a simple question I asked at the dinner table with a "What, honey?" that caught us both off guard. Embarrassed, we quickly resumed the regular family MO as if this term of endearment, spoken in a foreign tongue, had never been uttered.

Christmas at our house was similarly unsentimental. Presents came in boxes from Bamberger's, or J. C. Penney, or Sears, often with the price tags still attached. So there was no way I was going to give my mother the homemade piece of jewelry I'd made in my fifth-grade class only to have everyone stare at me, as if I were an alien who'd flown into our living room from another planet.

A month or two before the holidays, our teacher, Miss Rule, passed out to each of us a slice of a walnut shell. Mine was as ugly as all the others around the room, a dull hamster-brown color, about an inch long and a quarter-inch thick, with four main holes of different sizes connected by sinewy strands. It looked like a miniature model we might examine during science, maybe a replica of the human heart or something. But Miss Rule said this was a craft project. We were going use these walnut slices to make pins, which we could then give to our mothers for Christmas or Hanukkah.

Miss Rule was a popular teacher and usually had pretty good ideas, but that time I eyed her skeptically. She wasn't an art teacher. Did she really know what she was talking about? I had a hard time imagining that this ugly walnut shell could become a piece of jewelry and an even harder time imagining I'd give it to my mother for Christmas. As with so many other things teachers said through the years, I thought to myself, "Miss Rule has never been to *our* house." But always eager to please any teacher anytime, I played along.

The first step was to steep our walnut slices in a wood stain. As the stain set in, the walnut's color gradually transformed from dull, flat brown to a dark mahogany that penetrated every fiber of its inner chambers. The shellacking process the next day took a lot less time than the staining, and soon my walnut lived up to its luminous promise, glowing with the same rich wood tone as the console TV and stereo in our living room.

After I completed the final step, attaching a clasp to the less-perfect side of the walnut with Elmer's Glue so that it could be worn as a pin or a brooch, I swelled with pride, having created a real piece of jewelry. But I also felt a creeping anxiety. Now what? I wasn't really going to give this thing to my mother, was I?

On the afternoon we could take our pins home, I walked home from school, riddled with indecision about what I was going to do with it. Maybe I would keep it in my desk drawer along with other pieces of buried artwork I wasn't quite ready to part with yet. Or maybe I'd just drop it in the kitchen garbage can when no one was looking. But when I came through the door and saw my mother struggling with her laundry basket as she walked up from the basement, I reached into my pocket and, as if by some uncontrollable impulse, held out the pin. Feigning as casual an affect as I could muster, I said, as if it were an afterthought:

"Oh, Mommy—we made these in school. It's a pin made out of a walnut."

"Oh!" Sophie said, setting down her laundry basket and then examining the pin I placed in her palm with my eyes averted.

Barely getting the ~~~~ "It's ~~~~."

I didn't know what my mother really thought of the pin—or of me for having given it to her—so I stayed out of her way for the rest of the afternoon. I certainly didn't want to look at her face and relive the awkwardness of it all. I just sat in my room alone until dinner, letting "it's pretty" play in my head like a skipped record, over and over.

~

That year, Halloween fell on a Sunday, which meant that my mother needed to buy Halloween candy along with all our other groceries during her regular weekend shopping. Every Saturday morning, Sophie would open all the kitchen cabinets and look through the refrigerator to plan her weekly trip to ShopRite. As far as I can remember, she never made a list but instead kept the whole thing in her head. Feeding a large family was to her, I guess, like riding a bicycle—after you've done it for a while, you don't need an instruction manual. While my mother played out this weekly ritual, I performed my own—loitering around the kitchen and waiting for an invitation to tag along to ShopRite so that I could push the cart, play housewife, and check out the latest cleaning products and quick-and-easy foods by Betty Crocker and Pillsbury I saw advertised on daytime television. I knew what my mother thought about the fact that I wanted to go grocery shopping with her every Saturday while the normal boys in the neighborhood were out fishing or playing football, but it was a force beyond my control. While waiting to figure out which of my sisters was going to drive her to the store, Sophie always gave in to my longing, and I'd hop into the backseat of the car feeling a combination of glee and shame.

The Somerville ShopRite in those days was small, crowded, and poorly stocked. (The cramped space that housed it is now a liquor store, and a new mega-sized ShopRite has sprung up on the other side of town.) On a Saturday morning, you often had to follow someone to their car just to get a shopping cart, a process that could take up to fifteen minutes. But Sophie thought ShopRite had the best prices, and when you were feeding a lot of kids, that mattered.

On this particular Saturday, we got an especially late start. Sophie was muttering to herself about how nobody wanted to help her anymore, and she was frustrated and fidgety because she knew the store would be badly picked over by the time we got there. But as a nondriver with a disappearing husband, she also knew she was powerless against my sisters' increasingly busy schedules. And as much as I wanted to, I was too young to drive and therefore powerless to help.

We finally got to ShopRite around 3:30, and it was even more jammed with people than in the mornings. Trying to transform my presence from that of pathetic tagalong to useful shopper's assistant, I scoured the parking lot looking for people headed to their cars so that I could snag a cart the minute somebody finished putting the last bag of groceries into their trunk. By the time I made it to the produce section with the cart I'd commandeered, Sophie—who always prided herself on her ability to make decent meals on a tight budget—was already deflated, slouching near the bins of bruised fruits and vegetables that were left over this late in the day.

As we worked our way through the store, we found the shelves even barer than usual. And when we got to aisle 9, where they kept the candy, our Halloween options were very few. All the well-priced bags of fun-size candy were gone, people having taken advantage of what had obviously been a great sale. What was left were a few six-packs of large Hershey bars and double Reese's cups that cost a lot more than my mother was prepared to spend on Halloween candy. The knit in her brow betrayed how much it stressed her out to have to spend this kind of money on a bunch of strangers' kids. But she knew a lot of trick-or-treaters would come to our door, so we had to be prepared. Since my mother had already had to humble herself to get one of my sisters to take her to ShopRite, she'd be damned if she was then going to ask to be dropped off at Acme or Grand Union just to buy Halloween candy.

"I don't know, I don't know," Sophie said, looking alternatively at the heavens and at me for help in solving her dilemma. Secretly, I was thrilled at the prospect of the neighborhood kids thinking we were rich if we gave out candy bars this size, but I knew better than to voice this sentiment. Instead, I shrugged my shoulders and tried to be an ally while Sophie struggled to make a decision. Finally, with her signature sigh of resignation, she frisbeed the candy packages into the already full cart two and three at a time. We finished our shopping, rang up all the

Sophie stored the million-dollar candy in one of the upstairs bedrooms, put the rest of the groceries away, and started getting ready for dinner, probably the usual Saturday night special of hamburgers and frozen, crinkle-cut French fries. By this point she'd no doubt forgotten all about the frustration she'd felt at ShopRite a few hours before, but I hadn't. Silently, the Halloween candy that took up half my mother's weekly food budget called me upstairs, and it didn't take me long to find it in the cubbyhole underneath one of the eaves of our house, where she usually hid presents she didn't want us to see until Christmas.

I pulled the bags of candy out from their hiding place and held the packages in my hands. I didn't know why I was here or what I would do now that I'd found this candy. Was I going to tear open the packages and start devouring these oversized Hershey bars and double-packed Reese's cups that the greedy, ungrateful teenagers who would come to our door didn't deserve? Then, inexplicably, tears started to form in my eyes. Before long, I was stifling sobs that came from deep down in my chest and stomach, a flood of tears falling on the candy packages' crinkly cellophane wrappers like a burst of unexpected rain.

The best sense I can make of this moment now is that I saw, in this minor defeat over Halloween candy, the sum of all the losses and disappointments of my mother's life, or at least as many as a ten-year-old could fathom. As maybe all children of unhappy mothers do, the thing I wanted more than anything was to make things right for her, to see her smile, to fix her life. Yet even when it came to something as simple as buying Halloween candy, my mother couldn't win. And I couldn't do anything to help.

"BennyMichaelThomas!!!" Sophie hollered up the stairs, reducing, as always, our three names to one. "Come on! Supper's ready!"

~

Later that fall, Sophie went on a rare night out with Aunt Helen, who lived with Uncle Ted. (Ted and Helen, Yosh's unmarried brother and sister, lived next door in the house that had been my grandmother's until her death.) Helen played bingo one, two, sometimes three nights a week at whatever Catholic church or fraternal lodge in the area was having a bingo night. In church basements and function halls around the county, she'd chain-smoke her unfiltered Pall Malls, swear up a blue streak at her chronically unmarked cards, shoot daggers at the caller through her cat's-eye glasses, and never win a dime. Sometimes just to get Aunt Helen going, we kids would ask her the day after a bingo night, "So—did you win?" The answer was always the same: "*Win?* Win *shit!*"

In comparison to Helen, Sophie lived a demure life, at least as far as anyone who didn't hear her yelling at my father every night could tell. She'd given up smoking and regular bingo-playing years before, avoided the worst curse words except when Yosh drove her to use them, and hardly ever left the house, living vicariously through the characters she watched on television. So when Helen coaxed my mother out to bingo on a Saturday night, it was an event. Sophie put on the brown fake fur all middle-aged women seemed to have in the 1970s—which my sisters had to convince her to get after she'd insisted she had no place to wear it—got into the passenger seat of Helen's Chevy Nova, and rode off for a girls' night on the town.

Once the ten o'clock news started on TV, I knew my mother and aunt would soon be back with news of the bingo winnings. Rooting for the underdog, as I always did when watching one of my daytime game shows, I fantasized that my mother would waltz through the door with a big smile on her face and a wad of cash in her hand. At around 10:30, the reek of secondhand smoke from the bingo parlor filled the house, and I ran into the kitchen to hear the night's tally. Helen, as anyone could have predicted before the evening began, won shit. Sophie, it turned out, also won shit.

Helen, still steamed about her lousy cards, the lousy caller, and her "lousy friggin' luck every friggin' time," stamped out her Pall Mall in our kitchen and went home. Sophie, never having expected the big jackpot to come her way, looked tired but also a little uplifted just for having gotten out of the house for a few hours. As she reached to take off her coat and hang it in the closet, I spotted the walnut pin attached to the collar. Its deep brown had blended in with that of the fake fur so well that I hadn't even noticed it when she left. It was the first time I'd seen her wear it, and it obviously hadn't had much of an effect as a good-luck charm. But it did look sort of pretty there, I thought, as I smiled in the top bunk, saying nothing to Benny about the piece of homemade jewelry he never even knew existed.

5

Role Models

Middle school was going to be different. This wasn't just a promise I made to myself—it was a fact.

First, there was the location. After having spent six years trapped within the tiny imaginary circle surrounding Van Derveer Elementary School and our house, which you could probably draw with a single piece of fat chalk, I'd be where all the teenage action was—in downtown Somerville, a full mile away from Lincoln Avenue.

Second, there was the building. Because all the classrooms at the middle school were on the periphery, the hallway traffic all flowed in one direction, counterclockwise, as indicated by orange, card-stock arrows posted high above the doors and lockers. The orderliness of it all seemed very serious and adult to me, and I imagined scenes of teen intrigue playing out every hour between classes. It would be just like *Room 222*, a "dramedy" I watched with hushed reverence and anticipation over the summer that depicted the triumphs and traumas of an ethnically diverse group of Los Angeles high school students, all with big, cool hair, played by actors pushing thirty. The show's plots involved romantic conflicts, antiwar protests, drugs—situations far more compelling than the childish sports competitions of elementary school. Maybe I would have a girlfriend, become a hippie, join the middle school peace movement. Who needed a ribbon from Field Day?

Third, there would be a whole new group of kids, at least half the sixth grade, who wouldn't even know me. Van Derveer was one of two feeder schools to the middle school, with Central being the other, more diverse one. Whereas Van Derveer's population ranged from lower middle class (mostly Catholic) to upper middle class (mostly Jewish and Protestant), virtually all white, the students from Central ran the gamut: wealthier kids who lived in the big West End Victorians, Black and Puerto Rican kids who lived above storefronts or south of Main Street; poor White kids who lived in publicly subsidized garden apartment complexes. I didn't understand all these segregated community dynamics at

at Van Derveer, and if I could be different, too, maybe everything could be different.

Fourth and most important, I found out over the summer that my teacher's name would start with "Mr." I'd never had a male teacher before or spent any significant amount of time with an adult male other than my father, so I had no idea how it was all going to play out.

One thing that threw a bit of a wrench into my *Room 222* fantasy was that sixth-graders were all relegated to the annex, a wing off to the side with an L-shaped hallway—sadly, traffic had to flow in both directions—and where you still had one teacher for most of the day except for gym, reading, math, and "technology," a seventies mishmash of science, woodshop, and creative writing all in one course. So in some ways, it would still be a lot like elementary school. But once Mr. Farello walked into the room, it felt like a whole new world.

"Hey, guys! Don't look so glum. It's only ten months!" he teased us on the first day of class, with a smile I decided was at least partly directed toward me. He then told us he was one of the middle school football coaches, which for a moment made me very, very nervous. But if Mr. Farello had any dislike for unathletic boys like me, he didn't show it.

Mr. Farello was tall, well over six feet, with curly blond hair, seriously large glasses, and a pale complexion that gave the impression he stayed inside all day and read books. Probably in his mid-thirties, he was younger than my father but older than my brothers. His sensitive, gentle manner and the air of braininess he carried with him gave me my first image from real life of the kind of man I could become when I grew up. He wasn't a sitcom dad or a game show host; he was a real adult male who would be a part of my life every day. He was smart, he was kind, and where other kids may have seen just a teacher at the front of the room, I saw hope.

I didn't have a crush on Mr. Farello, but I *really* wanted him to like me, and Kevin Rice swooped in on this fact like a bird of prey from day one. A short, scrawny kid with pale skin and a mop of dark brown hair, Kevin was one of the least threatening-looking boys in my class. If he were a dog, he'd have been the runt of the litter. But what Kevin lacked in physical stature he made up for in intensity of hatred, all of it apparently directed toward me.

"Oh, Mr. Farello, I know, I know," Kevin mimicked my voice and hand gestures as I answered a question on the first day of school. Then under his breath, in a sneer I would recognize over the telephone to this day, one more word: "Faggot."

I'd certainly been called names before, and I'd heard the f-word muttered by boys at Van Derveer under circumstances that often made me wonder if it had to do with me. But Kevin's delivery was different. There was bile in it, something primal, diseased, even sexual. It turned me inside out, brought my faggot guts to the surface for all to see. And it was constant—twenty, thirty, maybe forty times a day. Compared to Kevin, the boys at Van Derveer had been mere amateurs.

Even if I kept my hand down to avoid Kevin's glare, he found ways to assault my not-even-formed-yet sexuality every day, every hour. We got a lot of group work in Mr. Farello's class, which meant a lot of moving around the room and a lot of opportunities for Kevin to sidle up next to me:

"You fag, you fucking faggot, you queer, you're a fucking queer faggot."

Pretty soon it didn't matter what words Kevin used or what order he put them in. He had me where he wanted me. Now I was much more than the sissy I'd walked into the room determined not to be. I was the class faggot.

Mr. Farello heard Kevin's attacks on me much of the time. He'd look at me with sad eyes, then just go on with the class. Maybe he felt sorry for me and didn't want to draw any more attention to the situation; maybe he didn't know what to say. Or maybe Kevin intimidated him, too. For all of Mr. Farello's niceness, Kevin was twice as mean. One of them was going to set the tone for my first year of middle school, and it didn't take me long to figure out it wasn't going to be Mr. Farello.

∼

Several afternoons a week we had our eclectic "technology" course, for which our entire class went next door to Mr. Charner's larger classroom and kids from both classes worked in stations on various projects—a group in this corner cutting wood with a saber saw, others over here working on a science experiment. I didn't trust Mr. Charner from the start. I saw his squinty green eyes glare at me whenever I did or said ~~something a little effeminate, and I doubted he would ever take my side~~ ~~in a dispute with Kevin. He wasn't like Mr. Turine, who even if he~~ thought you were a complete fag wouldn't let on. So in this group of fifty or so kids, I would need allies.

One afternoon, I found myself sitting in the creative writing area near Terrence Hall and Richard Bates, two Black boys who had gone to Central and whom I only knew from a few previous sessions of the technology class. Terrence was tall, wiry, and lean, with a quiet air of toughness and intensity about him. Richard was short, handsome, and affable, Terrence's friendly, easygoing sidekick. They generally kept to themselves in this mostly White class, and I could tell they weren't particularly interested in doing a creative writing assignment with a faggy White kid from Van Derveer.

The usual task for creative writing, which was a one-day activity you could do if you were between longer projects in science or woodworking, was to listen to a song on the tape recorder, then write an essay about what you thought the lyrics meant. It was 1970s, touchy-feely pedagogy in its purest form, and it left most kids totally perplexed. Marcie Saunders got the Beatles song "Let It Be" once and just wrote "let it be, let it be, let it be, let it be . . ." all over the paper for forty-five minutes. She wasn't being a smartass; that was all she could come up with.

Just as I was about to hit the play button to find out what the assigned song was, Terrence and Richard started talking between themselves about music they liked. They named a lot of R&B songs and, to their surprise, I was familiar with most of them and started chiming in. Having grown up with six older siblings, my musical tastes were more adult than those of most of my peers, and I'd developed an early appreciation for things like the Beatles and Motown that prepared me well for this conversation. Terrence said he especially liked "Me and Mrs. Jones," a scandalous (for middle school) Billy Paul song about an extramarital affair. I started singing it softly, and Terrence and Richard suddenly got quiet:

> Me and Mrs. Jones,
> We got a thing goin' on . . .

By the time I got to the chorus, they were transfixed:

> Meeeeeeeee aaaaand—Mrs! Mrs. Joh-ou-ones!
> Mrs. Jones, Mrs. Jones, Mrs. Jones . . .

They cracked up at my bluesy treatment of these last lines—eyes closed, fading to near silence by the time I got to the last "Mrs. Jones." They asked me to sing it over and over, and I had absolutely nothing to show Mr. Charner at the end of the period. (I don't remember what the assigned song for creative writing was, but I'm pretty sure it wasn't "Me and Mrs. Jones.") Normally, the teacher-pleaser in me would have panicked about getting a zero for the day, but who cared? I had two new friends, one of whom I was pretty sure could kick Kevin Rice's ass in about three seconds.

The next day in technology, I made sure to pass by Terrence and Richard as our class entered Mr. Charner's room. They took the bait and started calling other kids over.

"Hey, Vanessa! Hey, Martin! Come 'ere!" Once an audience was assembled: "Michael! Sing Mrs. Jones! Sing Mrs. Jones!"

By now, I was embellishing my performance, like I was the guest star brought in to sing the week's slow dance number on *Soul Train* or *American Bandstand*. Picking it up at the third verse, I emoted:

> It hurts so much, it hurts so much inside.
> Now she'll go her way,
> And I'll go mine.
> Tomorrow we'll meet, the same place, the same tiiiiiiiiiiiiime!
> MEEEEEEEEEEEE AAAAAAAND
> MRS! MRS JOOOOONES!
> Mrs. Jones, Mrs. Jones, Mrs. Jones . . .

Wonder, laughter, applause. Not since my headline-reading days at Club Royale had I experienced so thoroughly the public's admiring awe.

⁓

We got back to Mr. Farello's room later that afternoon and I started singing "Me and Mrs. Jones" quietly to myself, hoping one of my classmates would notice and echo the accolades of the previous hour.

as many classmates as possible to hear, but quietly enough for it to fly under Mr. Farello's radar. "God, you sing that nigger shit like a girl. You're such a fag!"

I should have known Kevin had been watching me with Terrence and Richard next door—he watched everything I did. I stopped singing immediately, looked down at my desk, and started doing something, anything to end the moment and rush time onto another one.

The next few times we had technology, I walked by where Terrence and Richard were sitting, hoping to recreate the "Mrs. Jones" magic. Their greetings, especially Terrence's, grew more tepid as the days passed. Richard still smiled when he saw me, but he didn't stop to talk or invite me over to where they were sitting, taking the lead from his cooler friend. As all things in middle school do, the "Mrs. Jones" routine got old pretty fast, and Terrence and Richard didn't seem to have much interest in me without it.

Kevin, on the other hand, remained obsessed with me for the rest of the year. The situation came to a head one late-spring morning right before music class. As he did every week, Mr. Farello led us out of the sixth-grade annex and marched us double file all the way across the main middle school building, then down into the basement where our music teacher, Mrs. Evans, had her classroom. We were early for music this week, so we stood in the hall for an especially long time until the previous class came out. Outside Mrs. Evans's room, Kevin was getting particularly fidgety. Looking for something to do, he started in at me, seeming unable to control himself:

"Faggot, faggot, faggot, faggot, faggot, faggot," over and over, like a tic he couldn't stop if he tried.

Then with pokes at my shoulder and chest, more of the same: "Faggot, faggot, faggot, faggot . . ."

The physicalization of Kevin's taunts, which up to this point had been exclusively verbal, finally caused me to snap.

"Stop it!" I said loudly, surprising even myself.

Having never touched me before, Kevin then punched me straight in the gut, apparently for having had the audacity to speak up. Other kids saw it, Mr. Farello didn't, and nobody said a word.

Kevin was pretty satisfied with himself—satisfied enough to finally stop saying "faggot"—but he'd pushed me to a breaking point. The previous class walked out of the music room, and ours filed in and sat down. Music was usually one of my favorite parts of the week, but this time I didn't even mouth the words to whatever we were singing, because all I could think about was Kevin. By the time class was over, I had a plan.

"And then he punched me in the stomach—for no reason at all," I reported to Mr. Farello in a meeting I'd requested after school. It was the first time I'd ever complained to a teacher or to anyone about being harassed, but I still faked ignorance about the reason why Kevin attacked me. I left out all the stuff about "faggot, faggot, faggot, faggot," the real heart of the matter. I didn't even think about making that word part of the story. Mr. Farello looked at me with his sad eyes, nodded, listened. I could tell his heart went out to me, but whereas that might have meant a lot at the beginning of the year, now it meant nothing.

Kevin didn't lay another hand on me during the few weeks of school that remained, so maybe Mr. Farello really did have a talk with him at some point. But Kevin's verbal gnawing at my psyche continued all the way up to the end of June. I never complained about it to Mr. Farello again—there just didn't seem to be any point. And just as in the situation with Mrs. Finch, I never mentioned it to anybody at home either. How do you tell your family that you've let another kid call you "faggot" hundreds of times, every day for the entire school year, without sounding like the very thing he calls you? And besides, my parents had plenty of their own problems.

~

The only thing on Lincoln Avenue louder than Sophie and Yosh's late-night shouting matches were Sophie and Yosh's late-night shouting matches in the summer. With the windows open to the screens, the "goddamns" this and "shits" that came into Benny's and my room at not one but two frequencies: one a muffled bass reverberating through the floorboards, sheetrock, and insulation, the other a more distant but clearer treble—traveling out of my parents' window, through the summer air outside, and into our wood-paneled sanctuary upstairs.

After George, Donna, and Larry had all gotten married and fled the

them in Larry's old room, the only upstairs space in our dormered Cape Cod with a ceiling tall enough to fit them. In addition to feeling more like teenagers in an upstairs bedroom, Benny and I hoped we'd get away from the downstairs din, and it helped to a point when the weather was cold and every window and door was shut tight. But in the summer, it didn't matter where we were—we might as well have all been in one room.

"I'm sick and tired of this goddamn bullshit!"

"*You're* sick and tired? The hell you are, you goddamn son of a bitch."

My parents' bedtime conversations, in both their predictability and audibility, bore an ironic resemblance to those on *The Waltons*, a CBS drama I loved about a family with seven children living in rural Virginia during the Great Depression. It almost always seemed to be summer on *The Waltons*. People hardly ever wore coats, and the windows were apparently open at bedtime because everyone, including the TV audience, could hear the family discussions that sprang up spontaneously before they all fell asleep.

Every Thursday, *The Waltons* would end with a night exterior of the house and one of the kids asking a question about the meaning of life, love, or God, which Mama or Daddy always answered with the perfect piece of folk wisdom. This would be followed by a labyrinthine series of good nights and, finally, the shutting off of a light and peaceful slumber while the crickets chirped on Walton's Mountain:

Good night, John-Boy.
Good night, Elizabeth. Good night, Daddy.
Good night, Son. Good night, Mary Ellen.
Good night, Daddy. Good night, Mama.
Good night, Mary Ellen. Good night, Jim-Bob.

Good night, Mama. Good night, Erin.
Good night, Jim-Bob. Good night, Ben.
Good night, Erin. Good night, Jason.
Good night, Ben. Good night, everybody.

Life on *The Waltons* wasn't a completely endless summer, though. My favorite episode was the series pilot, a Christmas story called "The Homecoming" in which the entire family waits on Christmas Eve for the father, John, who has had to leave the mountain to find work in a distant town. This forces his eldest son, fifteen-year-old John-Boy, to take on the role of man of the house—trudging through the snowy woods with his grandfather to find a Christmas tree, disciplining the younger children as they argue over what decorations should go where.

John-Boy was a comfort to me because he was a new kind of teenage TV protagonist. He was a bookish, sensitive misfit, not a popular jock like all the sitcom boys who, by middle school, I was starting to figure out I'd never be like. In the nine years *The Waltons* was on the air, I don't think John-Boy was ever shown playing a sport. Instead of being muscular and athletic, he was smart and sensitive—and he had a side of himself he couldn't reveal to the rest of the world.

"The Homecoming" was as much a coming-of-age story as a Christmas tale, and a lot of it revolved around John-Boy's secret wish to become a writer, an ambition for which he feels great shame because of his family's lack of money and his father's expectation that he'll "learn a trade." Much to his mother's dismay and consternation, John-Boy spends a lot of time locked in his bedroom, writing in a journal he keeps stashed under his mattress. When his mother, Olivia, finally confronts him about his secretive behavior, demanding to know what he does "behind that locked door" all the time, John-Boy nervously pulls his writing tablet from under the mattress and opens his heart:

"You know what's in that tablet, Mama? All my secret thoughts. How I feel and what I think about."

A stunned Olivia sits beside John-Boy on his bed, in awe of the son she now realizes she hardly knows. She pats his leg and assures him they'll talk about college and his writing aspirations "another time." The more pressing matter this Christmas Eve is that news has arrived on the wireless of an accident on the bus route Mr. Walton was to have taken home for the holiday. Olivia's worry has turned to panic, and she sends John-Boy into the snowy night to find his father, an odyssey that represents his passage into manhood.

~

I don't remember much about our own Christmases during this period

Thomas, and me—with the arrival of the Sears Wish Book in the early fall. Our task, as assigned by Sophie, was to make a list of exactly what we wanted, note the item, price, and catalog page number, then make sure it didn't add up to more than our allotted budget of thirty dollars each. The piece of loose-leaf notebook paper on which I wrote my Christmas list stayed in my desk drawer through weeks of revisions as I feverishly flipped through the catalog pages, dog-eared by early October, and was a crumpled mess of cross-outs and price calculations by the time I made my final submission in November.

Other than bringing home his paycheck from the paint factory, which was the foundation of our gift budgets, Yosh had nothing to do with Christmas. After setting our artificial tree in the stand, my father would walk away and essentially disappear for the rest of the holiday season, leaving all shopping, wrapping, cooking, and decorating to my mother and us kids. My father's absence from the Christmas planning was a blessing considering the austere views he had about what the holiday should be like for children. At Christmas, my sober and practical mother and my good-time-Charlie father switched roles, and for reasons I never quite understood Christmas did not bring out the festivity one might have expected from the otherwise sentimental Yosh. He thought my mother's annual indulgence of us with toy requests from the Sears catalog was frivolous, and every year he threatened to take over and buy us all "rain gear"—slickers, galoshes, and umbrellas—to open in front of the tree on Christmas morning. Luckily for us, following through on threats was never Yosh's strong suit, the *Wish Book* lists prevailed, and for most of the holiday season my father was nowhere to be seen.

~

In the only holiday memory I have from my middle school years, I'm twelve years old. I'm sitting in front of the TV with Sophie on Christmas night, hours after the leftover ham, kielbasa, Jell-O mold, and green bean casserole have all been put in the refrigerator. My older siblings have dispersed to their respective spouses and boyfriends and left Benny, Thomas, my parents, and me at home to feel the full weight of the post-Christmas letdown.

Thomas is asleep, Benny's upstairs doing I don't know what, and Sophie and I are watching a made-for-TV movie called *Home for the Holidays*. It's a barnburner mystery in which Sally Field realizes that one of her family members, all of whom are gathered for Christmas, is a murderer and now wants to make her the next victim.

After revealing whodunit, ABC switches over to *Marcus Welby, MD*, my mother's favorite primetime show. She has a crush on Robert Young, who plays the avuncular Dr. Welby, and an even bigger one on James Brolin, the younger, hotter Dr. Stephen Kiley. Despite my interest in soap operas, not to mention the handsome, motorcycle-riding Dr. Kiley, I find *Marcus Welby* boring, and my mind starts to wander. Suddenly it dawns on me that it's been a long time since I've seen my father.

"Where's Daddy?" I ask Sophie, puzzled because his car is still in the driveway.

"I don't know," she says, shaking her head. How the hell should she know? Why should she care? And why in Christ's name would I ask this question in the middle of her program?

But I'm unnerved by the eerie silence in the house, so I take a walk around. My father isn't in the kitchen. He isn't in bed. He isn't upstairs. Then I notice the basement light on and open the door. As I round the corner at the bottom of the cellar steps, I find Yosh in the same spot where I used to find Larry's deer carcasses hanging from the ceiling. He's made a loop with a cheap brown extension cord, like the kind you can get at a dollar store, and is tying it around one of the water pipes above him.

"Ya see what Daddy's doin'?" he asks me, holding up his makeshift noose. "That's it. I've had it. Nobody gives a shit. Nobody cares."

"I care," I say, not sure whether I really mean it. And apparently, he isn't sure either, because he just keeps on tightening the cord as if I haven't said a thing.

Now I realize that trying to talk him down, like I've seen people do on television when someone is standing at the edge of a tall building, isn't going to work in this real-life situation. So I take the only action I've ever known.

"Mommy!" I yell, while running back up the basement stairs. "Daddy's down the cellar with an extension cord. He says he's gonna hang himself."

then rolls her eyes and casts

going to get up off the couch to do anything about

attitude because she's probably right—he's just carrying on. Plus, there's no way our skinny water pipes could hold his weight, is there? But I feel drawn back down to the basement anyway, just to make sure my father doesn't end up swinging from the plumbing while my mother and I are watching *Marcus Welby, MD*.

I open the cellar door and walk down the first step or two, and I see Yosh walking up toward me. As we pass on the stairs, we don't say anything to one another about the scene that took place thirty seconds before. I wonder if he'll even remember it the next day. Then, just like one of us kids, he goes straight to my mother, who sounds doubly annoyed that she has to deal with his theatrics while *Marcus Welby* is on.

"What the hell were you doing down there? Jesus Christ!"

"You dunno, Shoph. You dunno what I go through," Yosh says, his S's thick and his eyes filling with tears.

"I know. Boy, oh boy, do I know. You're always cryin' the blues."

I walk the rest of the way down the stairs and silently untie Yosh's noose, which is still hanging where he left it, looking both menacing and ridiculously inadequate. I stash the extension cord in a compartment of the wall where I know he won't find it, just in case the impulse to hang himself comes back, then go upstairs to get ready for bed. I have no idea what to think about the scene I've witnessed or how seriously to take it. All I know is that I'll never say a word about it to anyone, ever. If I do, I figure, everyone will just laugh at me and tell me I watch too many soap operas.

I put on my pajamas and turn out the light. As I lie under the covers, I hear more slurring and hollering coming from the living room:

"I'm tellin' ya, Shoph, I've had it. One of these days I'm gonna get outta here, you mark my words!"

"Mark *my* words! *Get* the hell outta here—see if I care! There's the door!"

I close my eyes and sigh. We've now returned to our regularly scheduled program. Lulled by the sounds of this familiar din, I drift off to sleep, just as soundly as if I lived on Walton's Mountain.

Goodnight, Mama. Goodnight, Daddy.

6

1   Romantic

As seventh grade approached, I thought about the return to school with a mix of feverish excitement and sinking dread. The *Room 222* fantasy of teenage intrigue while students autonomously changed classes every hour would finally be waiting for me. But so would Kevin.

I knew he wouldn't be in any of my classes. Seventh grade was the beginning of all-day academic tracking in Somerville, and having always been a teacher's pet, I would be in one of the accelerated groups while Kevin would no doubt be in one of the lower sections, probably the lowest. Yet at any hour, as I rounded any corner of the building, he could show up out of nowhere, muttering "faggot, faggot, faggot," just loudly enough for it to seep under my skin before I went to my next class.

As it turned out, I didn't see much of Kevin anymore. He didn't suddenly vanish like Sheila Feldman had in first grade—he just faded slowly from my consciousness. I knew he was around, but we hardly ever ran into one another and when we did, it was a fairly benign encounter. He might slink toward me on a chance passing in the hallway and glare with his withering sneer. But he must have realized that outside the captivity of Mr. Farello's classroom, I could just walk on by, so eventually he did too. Maybe Kevin figured, when you can't make someone's life miserable day in and day out, what's the point of trying to do it at all? Maybe he found a new victim to prey on, or maybe he just grew up a little.

Without worries about Kevin dominating my life, I found a new obsession to occupy my thoughts every minute. Seventh grade was the height of the "going with" phenomenon at Somerville Middle School, a preteen form of dating in which you claimed a member of the opposite sex as your boyfriend or girlfriend and announced to the entire school that you were "going with" that person "4-ever"—that is, until you broke up, an equally public declaration that became the talk of the entire school. Going with someone was an exclusive arrangement that consisted of holding hands in the hallway, writing the other person's name all over your notebook (or both of your names with a plus sign inside a big heart), and the occasional kiss before a class, which varied in length and tongue involvement according to how sexually advanced you were. There was little actual dating involved unless somebody's parents dropped you off and picked you up at the movies or the bowling alley. It was mostly an in-school coupling, a Monday through Friday, 9-to-3 relationship. And it didn't take me long to find the girl I wanted to ask to go with me.

Sidney Auerbach was different from any girl I'd ever met. She had the longest hair I'd ever seen on a girl—straight, medium brown, and well past her waist. Her skin was porcelain white and her eyes deep blue, not pale like most blue eyes but dark, like a clear, late afternoon sky. She had a breezy way about her, always smiling and flinging her hair back, which she had to do anytime she wanted to sit down. And she wore the prevailing unisex middle school fashion, plaid flannel shirt and white painter pants, with just the right mix of femininity and androgynous nonchalance.

Sidney was in the accelerated learning group, too, so except for gym we were in class together all day. Whenever she said hi to me, or read aloud from whatever book we were studying in English, or walked across our math classroom to sharpen her pencil, my insides tingled. But my favorite thing about Sidney was her handwriting. It was curvaceous and feminine, but without all the extra hearts and circles a lot of other girls used, which I found sappy. Whenever I passed Sidney's desk, I'd glance over at whatever essay or worksheet was in front of her. Or, if she was writing a note to one of her friends, I would just gaze at it—not to read what she was writing, but just to imagine the notes she'd write about me soon and how my name and hers would look on our notebooks, penned in her beautiful, loopy cursive.

~

"You like Sidney, don't you?"

Todd, one of the boys at my lunch table, blindsided me with this question one day in the late fall, after I'd already spent a couple of months trying to muster the courage to ask Sidney to go with me.

Our table consisted of an odd assortment of misfits. James Bannister,

Todd was Bannister's best friend from elementary school, a handsome peacock of a seventh grader, the first boy I knew at school whose hair had highlights. Then there was Melvin, a heavy-set, frat boy of a twelve-year-old who loved gross-out humor. Once you put your food on the table, you'd better not get up to use the water fountain, go to the bathroom, or talk to anybody at another table unless you were finished eating. Otherwise, Melvin might taunt you with disgusting reports about how he'd contaminated your lunch while you were gone.

"I spit a hocker in that sandwich," Melvin would chortle after I'd had the bad judgment to get in line for a carton of milk, his performance often just convincing enough for me to throw away half my lunch uneaten.

An even odder match for the rest of us was Greg, a handsome Black kid who was both a football and track star and probably could have sat at any number of tables in the room. Why he chose to eat lunch every day with three of the more effeminate White boys in the seventh grade plus Melvin, a misfit of a different sort, remains a mystery to me. Greg's and my conversations mostly centered around Wednesday debriefings of the show *Good Times*, a Tuesday night sitcom we both followed about a poor Black family who lived on the south side of Chicago.

Todd's question caught me completely off guard. At first I said nothing, hoping the conversation would eventually just move back to one of Melvin's gross-out stories, *Good Times*, anything. But Todd wasn't giving up.

"Do you *like* Sidney?" he asked, a little louder this time. "I just want to know."

"Do you mean, like, *like* her? I don't know!" I answered, feigning a flabbergasted air as if the notion had never occurred to me.

Todd smirked, and the other three stifled grins that suggested they'd love to know the answer to Todd's question, too.

"I don't know. I don't know how I feel. I guess I never really thought about it."

Suddenly it was clear that my secret crush wasn't so secret. People were talking about the fact that I liked Sidney—maybe *she* was even talking about it—and the longer I did nothing, the worse it looked. The lunchtime conversation jolted me—into an even more calcified state of inaction. More weeks went by. I watched Sidney flick her hair and toss her head back when she laughed. I imagined holding her hand in the hallway and keeping her warm with my jacket at the high school football games while we sipped hot cocoa on the bleachers. I pictured "Sidney and Michael" hearts on both of our notebooks. But I did nothing about it, and I had no idea what was holding me back.

As the year wore on, conversation at the lunch table moved on to new topics, like the outdated, black-and-white sex ed movies we now had to watch in health class. Greg and I continued our weekly debriefings of *Good Times*, which lost a little steam once the season moved into reruns. Then Todd brought up Sidney's name again at the lunch table. This time he went on and on about how Sid said this and Sid did that and about he and Sid went to the movies the other day.

With a rock in my stomach, I asked, "Are you and Sidney—?"

"Oh! Yeah. I'm going with Sid now. You didn't know?" he tossed off. "I thought everybody knew."

"No," I said, barely managing a phony smile. "That's great."

He continued with Sid and him blah blah blah, then Sid blah blah blah. I couldn't even hear what he was saying anymore because my insides were screaming, "It's Sidney, not Sid! Sid is a man's name!"

But what business was it of mine? He was going with her now, and he could call her whatever he wanted. And if I needed any confirmation of this fact, I saw it when we returned to class, right on Sidney's notebook. Written along the edge of the spiral, in a big, Bic-pen heart, she had written: "Todd + Sid, 4-ever."

~

One spring Monday morning, I arrived at school a little later than usual. Already gathered in a corner to the right of the front door were Bannister, Todd, and a few other kids. Before I could even get in three words about what I'd watched on TV—always my default topic of conversation—Todd got right to the main headline, which everyone had obviously already been talking about before I arrived.

"Well, you can try for Sidney now," he said, looking right at me and waiting for my reaction. My heart leapt, but then I wondered if he was playing a cruel joke.

"What do you mean?"

"We broke up over the weekend," Todd said dismissively, as if it were all just a childish game he'd suddenly outgrown. "We both decided—just—it wasn't working out."

Then the bell rang and we all walked into school. My head was spinning with plans for the life Sidney and I would share as soon as I waited a respectable amount of time to ask her to go with me. Her heart might be broken, I thought, so I should tread lightly. Then I saw Sidney in class. She was chatting, tossing her hair back, laughing just like before, even with Todd. Maybe I wouldn't have to wait very long after all.

~

"May 11th!" said Señor Rivera, the Spanish teacher I had for homeroom, as he read from the announcement sheet one spring morning with a gleam in his eye. He knew this day would have great significance for many of us because it had just been announced as the date of the middle school dance. Every day from then on, Señor Rivera read the notice about the dance with flourish, and every day the sound of "May 11th" pushed the play button on a TV movie in my mind: Sidney and me holding hands as we walk into the gym for our first dance, Sidney and me slow dancing at the end of the evening to "Nights in White Satin" while our classmates "ooh" and "ah" at how adorably in love we are.

But first, I had to—once and for all—ask her to go with me. After still more weeks of paralysis, on May 10, the day before the dance, I tossed a note onto Sidney's desk during English, just as the window of opportunity was about to close. It was couched in cautious qualifiers and pre-apologies: "I wondered if maybe you would want to go with me" and "Sorry for asking in a note, but maybe could you let me know at the dance?" With a knowing smile, Sidney took the folded piece of paper, stuffed it in the pocket of her jeans, and said, "Thanks."

I walked home that afternoon with my mind spinning out ten thousand interpretations of the interaction that had taken place between us in English class, deliberations that preoccupied me all Friday night and into Saturday. Did Sidney's smile mean it was the invitation she'd been waiting for all year? Did she think it was cute that I was so shy I had to ask her in a note? Or did she think the whole thing was ridiculous and, of course, she would never go with me in a million years?

In the hours leading up to the dance, the movie in my head grew more colorful, its soundtrack now filled with slow dance numbers like "Stairway to Heaven" and Paul McCartney's "My Love (Does It Good)." In this longer, Technicolor version, Sidney's deep blue eyes gaze into mine, and she tells me she feels, for the first time in her life, what it's like to be truly loved. She puts her head on my shoulder during the last dance of the night, we walk hand-in-hand out of the gym, share a first tender kiss, then say a tearful goodbye.

~

"What time you gonna be done?" Yosh asked as he dropped me off in his brown Gran Torino outside the middle school gym.

"I don't know. 10:15, 10:30 . . ."

"*10:30!* I'm s'posed to pick you up *10:30?*"

"It's a *dance!* It isn't even over until 10 o'clock!" My heart was beating in my eyeballs by now, and the last thing I needed before walking into the dance was to get into an argument with my father. "If you don't want to pick me up, tell somebody else. Or I can walk."

"All right, all right."

Door slam.

Checking my hair and the fit of my best flannel shirt and carpenter jeans in the car window, I opened the door of the school, turned in my ticket, and walked toward the open door of the gym—and, it seemed, the rest of my life. A sea of faces surrounded me, many I'm sure I knew, but I couldn't see any of them because I was only looking for one. I circled the gym several times, but I didn't see Sidney anywhere. 7:15, 7:20, and she still wasn't at the dance. Finally, our classmate Susie walked up to me with a note in her hand.

"This is from Sidney. She asked me to give it to you," Susie said nervously.

I held the folded sheet of paper from Sidney's very own spiral notebook. It was the closest I had ever been to touching her, and my breath stopped when I saw my name, "Michael," written in her loopy cursive.

"Is she here?"

"Not yet." Susie said. "She might be coming later. I'm not sure."

"Thanks," I said, probably a little rudely, because I instantly broke away to the only private place I could think of, a stall in the boys' bathroom. I unfolded the note, which I had already written and rewritten in my mind a hundred times while walking down the hall, and my body flushed with heat as I took in the words:

> I don't know how to spell it.
> I don't know how to say it without hurting your feelings.
> I don't want to go with you.
> I just want to be your friend.

Boys came in and out of the bathroom for twenty, maybe thirty minutes while I sat in the stall, sobbed as silently as I could, and felt something collapse inside me. Maybe it was the hope I'd harbored all year for a life with Sidney, maybe it was hope for an image of myself I desperately needed to see reflected back at me. Maybe there was no difference. Whatever it was, now—in one evening, in four short lines written on a sheet of spiral notebook paper—it was gone.

Sidney's note did nothing to diminish my obsession with her. If anything, it intensified it, though the soundtrack to the movie in my mind shifted from "our song" ballads to those about misunderstood romantics and unrequited love. When we received the sonnet writing assignment that remains a staple of middle and high school English classes to this day, I penned overwrought quatrains with Sidney my secret muse:

> I wander through the streets on rainy nights,
> And reach to hold a hand that isn't there,
> Spend hours inside alone, without the lights,
> And mold the dark to draw your image near . . .

For two more years, I thought about Sidney constantly—or almost constantly. These were also the grades we began to use the locker room for gym. And when I wasn't thinking about Sidney, I was thinking about the boys who had gone through puberty early and whose tanned, muscled, man-like bodies were suddenly all around me, daring me to look. Seemingly overnight, some of the boys at school, especially those a grade or two ahead of me, were starting to look like men in the swim-wear pages of the Sears and Kmart circulars I now kept hidden under my mattress. I knew better than to betray as much as a glance in the locker room, and I also knew I should keep myself, and any evidence of the effect these boys had on me, covered up at all times. I indulged in these thoughts only within the privacy of my bedroom, where a side of me was emerging that I didn't quite understand well enough yet to fear.

In my mind, my locker room fantasies and stash of men's bathing suit ads had nothing to do with the names Kevin or Mrs. Finch or Gina Rosario or Sheila Feldman had called me. I wasn't that thing we had all heard Elton John was and were starting to gossip about at school. I was the hero of my own TV movie—misunderstood, his love unrequited, but still hopelessly determined to get the girl.

7

The Boy Who Didn't, Part 1

Six weeks into my eighth-grade year, on a Saturday night in mid-October, the weather was so warm we had the windows open to the screens, just like in summer. Indian summer was what we called this warm fall weather back then. True to form, Yosh wasn't home yet, even though it was well after midnight. Normally, he could have been at any number of his beer joints, but this time I knew—because his car was still in the driveway—that he was right down the street, three doors down from our house at the bar in the American Legion hall. At least he wouldn't be driving. But the close proximity of the Legion hall to our house also meant that his return would become a radio play for the entire sleeping neighborhood to hear. Maybe he'd be railing at whoever had pissed him off at the bar, or maybe he'd just be mumbling to himself, then announce his arrival with his classic slap of the back screen door.

"God damn you! Get the hell away from me!" or something like it is what I hoped I'd hear from my parents' room when Yosh tried to get into bed with Sophie after lumbering around the house for a few minutes. She'd be loud, strong, up to the old game, and they'd go at it again like a couple of prizefighters. But I hadn't seen or heard that side of my mother in some time. Instead, she'd been quiet lately and in bed for most of the past few weeks.

I didn't ask many questions about how or why my mother was sick. It started with loud, rattling coughing fits she seemed unable to control that went on for thirty, sometimes forty-five seconds. In hindsight, I realized these had been going on for months, maybe even years. But in the previous few weeks something had shifted. Now, in the aftermath of one of her coughing bouts, instead of going right back to house cleaning, or complaining about Yosh, or talking about the soap operas, Sophie grew quiet. After a while, my mother, who always seemed to be doing one chore or another to stay a step ahead of us kids, started spending most of the day in bed.

"Mommy has a cold," I said over and over to myself as I went on with my daily routine of going to school, watching TV, eating, doing homework, watching more TV, going to bed, and watching still more TV before going back to school the next day. Then the way this "cold" was being dealt with started to escalate. First, there were the visits to Dr. Byrne, our old-school family physician who worked out of a room in his house, and a diagnosis of "stress" that required no remedy except an effort to remain calm in the face of the chaos that was our family. (Dr. Byrne had known my mother for years, so he knew she had a hard-drinking husband and eight children to deal with.) Then, Dr. Byrne sent Sophie to the drugstore with a prescription for the same cherry- and metal-flavored syrup he gave to all of us when we had chest colds and the Vicks Formula 44 wasn't doing the trick.

After a couple of weeks, when things were getting worse instead of better, Donna took my mother to a specialist who worked out of the hospital. They came home with a green metal can that, other than the fact that it wasn't red, looked like a fire extinguisher. It had the brand name "Life-O-Gen" etched into it.

Mommy had pneumonia, Donna explained, a diagnosis that didn't scare me much. As an infant, I had had bronchial pneumonia, which I later referred to when I was old enough to talk as "bronco ammonia." (And since I couldn't remember having been sick, I actually thought it had something to do with horses or cleaning solution or both.) If I could survive bronco ammonia, so could Mommy. But we'd never had anything like the Life-O-Gen tank in our house. It haunted me with images of sick people, old people, coal miners with black lung disease, people who couldn't breathe on their own anymore because they'd smoked their lungs away.

Once the oxygen tank was set up in my parents' bedroom, I could never bring myself to go in or even walk by when my mother was there, because then I might see her using it. But when she got up to use the bathroom or had enough energy to make herself a piece of toast or a cup of tea in the kitchen, the Life-O-Gen would lure me into the room with its sinister call. I would stare at the green can, say its ominous name over and over to myself, and wonder what it all could mean.

~

On this oddly warm Saturday night, I awakened to the thought, "He's talking to himself again," as I heard Yosh coming down the sidewalk after his night at the Legion, his recognizable ramble moving closer and closer to the house. Then I heard other voices that were unfamiliar, young, and male.

"Get the hell out of my way. This is *my* house, you ffuckin'—"

I moved over to the screened window and peered out. Like a rubbernecker at a car accident, I didn't really want to witness the scene unfolding below me, but I couldn't look away. I made out four figures in the dark. The one flailing his arms in the air, throwing punches that didn't come anywhere near hitting their mark, was, of course, my father. After squinting for a few seconds, I realized that the other three were teenage boys or young men—late teens, early twenties at most. I didn't recognize these kids; they weren't from our neighborhood.

In the one or two minutes I peered through the screen, I pieced together the gist of the confrontation. The boys had been hanging out on our front lawn or in our driveway or maybe just on the sidewalk in front of our house when Yosh came staggering down the street. Maybe the kids had been drinking beer, maybe smoking weed, maybe doing nothing but talking. But Yosh, in a fit of fury that his territory had been invaded, started name calling, throwing punches, threatening to show them a thing or two with his fifty-six-year-old fists.

By the time I got to the window, this had obviously been going on for some time because Mr. Parker, our neighbor from behind who had probably already been in bed, was striding over to defuse the situation. He told the boys to go home, which they obligingly did, and tried to calm Yosh down. Yet even with the alleged intruders in retreat, Yosh couldn't stop hurling threats after them.

"You're just a bunch of fuckin' hoodlums. If I ever see yous here again I'll beat the fuckin' shit out a' yous!"

Even after the hoodlums were gone, Yosh still couldn't let it go. He was railing at Mr. Parker now, even more loudly than he had at the trespassers.

"I'll get those goddamn kids! They ever show up here again, I'll kill all a those mother ffuckin'—"

"It's okay. It's okay, John. You got the best of them," said Mr. Parker, the sober, conciliatory voice of reason, trying to quiet down this neighbor I was now sure he had seen and heard on these rampages many times. "Now you just relax and go inside. You got a sick wife in there, John, and you don't—"

You got a sick wife in there?

My heart began to race as I realized that news of my mother's illness had spread all over the neighborhood. Suddenly I knew that in houses down the block, people were saying things like, "Sophie has pneumonia. I hear she's bedridden." The kids I played with were chattering, "I heard Mrs. Sadowski is *really* sick."

Then time froze, and I held my breath for what I already knew, somewhere in the deepest core of me, was going to be Yosh's comeback to Mr. Parker. At volume one hundred, bellowing into the night air, he said:

"I don't give a goddamn if she dies!"

My father's words were so close to what I feared he would say that I wondered if somehow I had willed them myself. Right afterward, I questioned my hearing, my sanity, whether I was even awake. Could life really have become so much more terrifying in a single night?

～

The next morning, I woke up late, having taken hours to fall asleep the night before. All I could think about were the final words of Yosh's tirade, still reverberating inside me. As far as I knew, I was the only one in the house who had heard them, and I had no idea what to do about it. I'd never spoken up about much of anything before, but this time I needed to say something, didn't I? This was about life and death, and if I didn't defend my mother while she was so sick and unable to defend herself, what kind of a son was I?

Not quite having steeled my resolve yet, I walked downstairs. Yosh was sitting at the kitchen table staring out the window like he was waiting for someone, the Sunday *Daily News* and Newark *Star-Ledger* unopened in front of him. I walked past him in silence. Then Donna pulled up on the street alongside our house. Maybe I'd report to her what Yosh had said, I thought. Except for George, who now lived six hours away, she was the oldest. I'd let her handle it. But by the time Donna made it into the kitchen, Yosh's driveway scene wasn't even front-page news.

Donna, it turned out, was coming back from the hospital, where she'd taken our mother earlier that morning. Mommy had had a bad night, couldn't breathe, Donna said. She was doing a little better, but they wanted her admitted for tests, observation, something. Even though Yosh's words were now banging around in my head even louder than before, the idea of reporting them suddenly seemed unimportant, juvenile. Nothing my father had said or done mattered anymore. The only thing that mattered was that, for the first time since Thomas was born, our mother was in the hospital.

Later that afternoon, Donna and some of my other siblings were going over to the medical center. I couldn't even walk past my mother's room when she was lying sick at home with the Life-O-Gen tank. How could I see her in the hospital with tubes in her mouth and arms, machines beeping next to her bed, like when a character was hospitalized on one of our soap operas? When I asked Donna if I should come along, she said that it was probably best we didn't all go at once. Mommy was tired and needed to rest, she said. I could go tomorrow, she said. I didn't argue. I stayed home and watched TV.

～

The next day was Monday, so I went to school. I tried to concentrate on English and history and algebra, but all I could think about was what I was going to do that night, when my siblings would probably be going back to the hospital to see our mother. When I got in from school, Donna relayed a conversation she'd had with Sophie's attending physician.

"I don't want to paint a rosy picture, but I don't want to paint a black picture either," he had told her.

Those words became a new echo that bounced back and forth between my ears. What did they mean? That things were better? That things were worse? I had a mental image of what the rosy picture could look like—Mommy smiling, bursting out of her bed, coming home and getting back to the old routine as if nothing had ever happened. But what did the black picture look like, and why was the doctor even talking about that? I had no idea what to do with this new information, so I just did what I had done the previous day. I sat in front of the television. No one questioned me or even suggested I go to the hospital, and I wasn't sure my mother wanted to see me anyway. When you're the seventh of eight kids, it's easy to convince yourself that your own individual presence won't make much of a difference. Even now, I wonder if that might have been true.

~

Tuesday came. Was there news of a minor rally? A slight decline? I don't remember. All I remember is that I didn't go to the hospital.

~

The next time I remember is Wednesday around 3:30.

It's still warm out, weirdly so for October. I'm walking down Lincoln Avenue toward our house, and as I approach our corner, I notice familiar cars, a lot of them, parked on the street: Mark's Volkswagen Beetle, Nancy's Chevy Vega, Donna's Monte Carlo. In the twenty seconds or so it takes for me to walk around to the back of the house, I invent a million scenarios for why this might be—a family event I forgot about, someone's birthday, maybe even helping Mommy get set up back at home. When the driveway comes into view, I see more cars parked in front of the pigeon coop: Larry's Pontiac GTO, Yosh's Gran Torino, Aunt Helen's Chevy Nova. It's the middle of the afternoon. Why is everyone here?

I walk through the back door, just like every day after school since kindergarten, through our wood-paneled kitchen, and toward the living room. Despite the lineup of cars outside and the voices I hear murmuring in the next room, I screw my consciousness into expecting the familiar: Mommy sitting alone on the sofa, folding laundry, watching *One Life to Live*. But the twenty-five-inch GE console in the corner is uncharacteristically dark and silent, and the living room is filled with people who shouldn't be there on a Wednesday afternoon: my three sisters, who all have full-time jobs, and George, who's now working his first post-MIT job on the far west side of Pennsylvania. George's wife, Liz, and their four-year-old son, GJ (George Jr.), are there, along with their month-old infant, Joshua, whom I have never seen before. Nancy is holding the baby, and my next tactic is to smile at this new family member and pretend that his arrival is the big news. *No one told me George and Liz were coming to visit! Everybody came over to see the new baby!* Nancy plays along for a second, looks at me and asks, "Isn't he cute?" But behind her weak smile at the infant in her arms, I can see she's been crying.

Then I notice Yosh behind me, sitting alone on one side of the two-person love seat along the banister. His eyes are blood-shot, the lids swollen and purple. He looks up at me and pats the seat for me to sit next to him. It's the tenderest gesture he's ever made toward me, and I want to spit in his face. But it's all happening so fast, I just sit down.

Yosh flops his arm around my shoulder, and I feel his entire body weight collapse against me, his whiskey-scented breath now right next to my nose.

"We'll get along," he blubbers. Then he starts to sob, uncontrollably, unable to say another word.

Yosh has still not provided any literal information about what's going on, so I take the opportunity to flip back into treating the whole scene as perplexing instead of blatantly obvious. Why do we need to *get along?* Get along *how?*

I look up, and my falsely uncomprehending eyes meet George's. He's the oldest, and he now knows he has to complete the task my father couldn't.

"Mommy died," he says quietly.

"Really?" I ask. One last attempt to craft some sort of alternative reality out of the overwhelming facts.

George nods. He can see none of it makes any sense to me given what I've been told so far.

"I guess Mommy had cancer, but she didn't tell anybody."

I feel a wave of something, nausea maybe, building up fast inside me. I stand up, extricate myself from Yosh's grip and George's stare, walk straight to the bathroom, and lock the door. Except I don't lean over the toilet. Instead, I look in the mirror, and now I know the wave inside me is something else. In an instant, it breaks, and my entire life as I've known it starts to choke out of my body in loud, gut-deep sobs.

Immediately, I jam a towel into my mouth, muffle the sound as best I can for the shame of it all. Even in this moment, I care about being the right kind of boy. And after fifteen or twenty minutes, when the wave finally starts to recede, I make a decision. I am never again going to let anyone, especially my father, see or hear me cry.

Eventually, my sobbing gives way to a silent fog that allows me to walk back out into the living room. Not looking at or talking to anyone, I walk straight through the room and exit as wordlessly as I'd entered. I head up the stairs to Benny's and my room. To my relief, he isn't there. Even though we've just been through exactly the same thing, I can't face him because our eyes might meet, and then what?

Once I close the bedroom door, I yearn to go further and further up more stairs that don't exist, anywhere, just somewhere else. But where is there to go where this won't be true? I look out the window and down onto the street. All I can see for what seems like miles are the familiar cars that aren't supposed to be there in the middle of the afternoon, but are.

The next few hours are a blur. I hear some talk about dinner downstairs. Neighborhood moms I can't face because they're still alive come to the door with food. Do they think a Bundt cake is going to make us feel like everything is okay? Or that if we eat enough baked ziti, our mother will come back?

Hours later, Benny and I are in our bedroom, not saying a word. Finally, I ask him if I can turn on our portable Magnavox, seeking the only place I can think of that might feel a little bit like home. When I flip the switch, the TV is tuned to Channel 7 and a sitcom called *That's My Mama*.

~

The next day, the drive to the afternoon viewing confirmed the television and radio media's deliberate attempt to mock me—and only me—in my solitary grief. As we rode to the funeral home in my sister Kathy's old Chevy Impala, she tuned the radio to the local top-forty station, WABC, as if it were just a normal car ride, like maybe we were all just going to school or maybe to the mall. The first song that came on was the Three Degrees ballad "When Will I See You Again?"

I felt certain I was the only one who got the irony of this or was even paying attention to the lyrics. I scrunched up tighter into the ill-fitting blue blazer I hardly ever wore. I let a few unvoiced tears well up in my eyes, but otherwise it was a silent, ten-minute ride to the place where my mother was to be laid out in an open casket, wearing the dress she was supposed to wear to Kathy's wedding three weeks later.

Our family drove over to the funeral home in multiple carloads, and most of my siblings had already arrived by the time our group got there.

When we walked in, a crowd was waiting in the front hall to sign the guestbook, and we had to push through this vestibule and around a corner to enter the viewing room where my mother's casket was. Most people immediately recognized us as "those poor kids" and got out of the way.

As my siblings started to enter the room one by one and go to the front to see our mother, I hung back, and then hung back some more. They were all in there now except for seven-year-old Thomas, who had been dropped off somewhere. With a neighbor? A cousin? Who remembers? Yosh was in the viewing room, too, apparently more or less behaving himself, because no one was talking about it.

As I inched around the corner and approached the room where my mother's coffin lay, I caught a millisecond glimpse of her, my first in almost a week. I saw the peach-colored mother-of-the-bride dress, the brown helmet-hair wig, the funeral home makeup job that made her look younger and prettier than I had seen her look in years. Except she was dead. My view of her lifeless body lasted for less than a second, and it lasted forever. In an instant, I saw confirmation not only of the fact that she was never coming back but also of all the ways I'd failed her. Whatever vague, vain hope I'd held onto that someday, maybe when I was older, I'd be able to fix my mother's sad life, now it was too late. The game was over, my mother had lost, and there was nothing I could do anymore to help her win. So I made the only rational choice I could make under the circumstances. I turned around and walked away.

I retreated to the entry hall and sat in a somber-looking armchair for a few minutes, making myself a target for the condolences of passersby that I barely acknowledged. Then I realized I could escape their gazes if I went downstairs to the basement, where I knew there was a bathroom. For what must have been long enough for people to notice, I disappeared from the wake, using the metal walls of a toilet stall to protect me from the truth outside. Then I heard a soft knock, and the door swung open an inch or two.

"Michael, are you in there?"

Between the voice and the familiar scent of perfume, I knew it was my cousin and godmother, Kate. To my single, childless godmother— who had always visited me or sent me a card with money in it on my birthday—I had always been a little bit special.

"I'll be right out," I yelled, only because it's what I always said when somebody knocked on the door when I was in the bathroom. And when I finally came out, Kate was waiting for me.

More than any of my sisters, Kate looked like a younger version of my mother.

"Can you sit down here with me for a minute?" she asked, gesturing to a small, upholstered bench that sat in the alcove between the women's and men's rooms.

Sitting next to the godmother who had come to find me, I broke my vow. The wave hit me again, and I cried, only more quietly this time. With my head on Kate's shoulder, I asked through my tears, "Why did she die? Why did she have to die?"

And with all the love she had for me, her only godson, in her voice, she answered, "It's God's will."

What does that mean? That she deserved it? That she was supposed to die? What kind of a God would want that to happen? I wanted to pull away, scream all this and more at Kate, but I didn't. Maybe I understood, even in my grief, that she was trying to help. And maybe in her own way, she did. Eventually, I let my crying spell wind down in her arms and allowed her to coax me back upstairs.

When we returned to the hallway, I contemplated trying to round the corner again into the viewing room. Then I realized that the image of my mother's lifeless body wouldn't have changed an iota. She'd still be lying there dead, so what was the point? I spent the rest of the afternoon walking back and forth between the bathroom and the outer hallway, my face stone, and never went inside.

That night we all returned to the funeral home for the evening visiting hours. I repeated my boycott of the room where the casket was and stayed in the outer hallway, with occasional trips to the bathroom, for the entire two hours.

A cousin of my father's I hardly knew looked at me, shook her head, and said to the woman standing next to her, "This one won't go no further." So now I wasn't just the boy whose mother had died—I was also the funeral home freak show. But I didn't care. I was never, ever going to enter the room where my mother was dead.

Later that night we were all back at Lincoln Avenue, the kitchen table now littered with more baked ziti, Bundt cake, cold cuts, and other foods people inexplicably eat large quantities of when someone dies. While most of the family and a few visitors stood crowded in the kitchen, I sat in a chair in the living room envisioning the next day, the day of the funeral. I tried to picture myself there, imagine a way I'd be able to get through it. As long as I didn't have to see her face, as long I could come in after the casket was closed, I could be there for my mother. Didn't I owe her that much? It was my last chance.

Just as I was contemplating all this, my four-year-old nephew, GJ, walked up to me with uncomprehending sadness in his eyes.

"Do you know what happened?" he asked, almost in a whisper.

"No, what?"

"Your mom died."

I smiled for a moment at his innocence, his blunt, unfiltered ability to see and name reality exactly as it was. And then I realized again, as if I didn't already know, that what this four-year-old child said was true. It really was that simple.

A little while later, it was clear that the older siblings, and maybe even my father in a moment of relative sobriety, had been discussing the way I'd been behaving at the funeral home. George walked over to the corner where I was sitting and crouched next to me. He spoke to me as softly as his son had a few minutes before.

"Uh, we were talking, and—you don't have to go tomorrow, you know."

"What do you mean?" I asked, already sensing where this conversation was headed.

"We're taking GJ and Thomas over to a lady's house, somebody Liz's mother knows. You can just go over there with them. If you don't want to go to the funeral, you don't have to. It's OK."

George was very careful not to use the word babysitter, but I knew that's exactly what this "lady" amounted to. I was nearly thirteen, and I was going to go to a *babysitter* with my seven-year-old brother and four-year-old nephew instead of to my mother's funeral?

"It's OK, I'm OK—I can go tomorrow."

"OK, well you don't have to decide now," George said. "Just think about it."

~

I spent the morning my mother was buried in the house of a woman I had never met and would never see again after that day. She smiled, spoke to me gently, and put game shows on the TV, someone obviously having told her I liked them.

I've attended enough funerals in my life that I can now piece together parallel stories for how that Friday morning played out for my older siblings and for me:

At 9:30, visiting hours start at the funeral home with the casket open. My father, brothers, and sisters are granted the final look. Then the lid is closed, and our mother's face is never seen by anyone again.

At 9:30, I play board games with Thomas and GJ on the babysitter's living room floor.

At 10:15, they're all at the Russian Orthodox Church, staring though tears at my mother's coffin while the priest delivers a service in which her name is barely mentioned.

At 10:15, it's snack time at the babysitter's house, white toast with grape jelly, or something like that.

At 11 o'clock, everyone arrives at the gravesite. The Russian priest says something incomprehensible over the flower-draped coffin. Then my siblings walk away from our mother for the last time, sobbing and holding one another while they return to their cars.

At 11 o'clock, I sit alone in the babysitter's living room while Thomas and GJ put together a puzzle at her kitchen table. I watch young Alex Trebek host *High Rollers*, a combination quiz show/craps game where a correct answer earns you a roll of the dice and the chance to win big money. I answer all of Alex's questions out loud and I don't shed a single tear, nor will I ever for the next seventeen years.

PART TWO

SILENCE

Lying is done with words, and also with silence.

—ADRIENNE RICH

8

The Boy Who Didn't, Part 2

Manville, New Jersey, the town just south of Somerville where my mother was born, grew up, graduated from high school, worked her first few jobs before marrying my father, and was buried at age fifty-one, was a town I always associated with death.

Until the 1980s, it was a major headquarters of Johns-Manville Corporation, one of America's leading distributors of asbestos-based products for construction: insulation, shingles, roofing—the things that make up the structure of a home. J-M closed the plant that gave the town its name around the time the use of asbestos for construction was banned, but the microscopic fibers had already taken their toll on the men and women who had worked there for decades—disposable, working-class lives of immigrants or the children of immigrants, mostly Eastern European, whose suffering no one would ever do anything to avenge. Maybe a bunch of class-action suits would be filed years later by the kinds of lawyers who advertise their services on television. There might be settlements of a thousand, maybe two, maybe even ten thrown to families who had watched fathers, mothers, sometimes sons and daughters gasp for breath, grow gray-faced and vacant, and slowly and painfully die making a living for their families.

Today, near the former site of the J-M plant in Manville stands a mega-sized Walmart, which sells baby furniture, tubes of toothpaste, and garden tools to the new wave of residents, many of them with roots in Latin America. Built on the energy of these families, Manville is again a quaint, even charming working-class community. There is little trace of the industry that killed so much of the town decades earlier or of the people who died, except perhaps in the memories of the nonagenarians who still attend the Russian Orthodox Church, where my mother's funeral took place in a language no one in my family could understand.

~

More than four decades later, I still have no idea how or why my mother died, her few years' work at the J-M plant during her twenties being one of many possible contributing factors I heard people speculate about, along with the smoking she had given up about ten years before, a viral or bacterial infection, and, as Dr. Byrne had diagnosed in the first few weeks of her illness, "stress." Yosh was in charge of the decision making after my mother's death, and he refused to allow an autopsy. What was the point, he said—it wasn't going to bring her back. So I still don't know if she had lung cancer, asbestosis, mesothelioma, pulmonary fibrosis, a viral or bacterial pneumonia that grew out of control, "stress," or some combination of these things. I don't know if, as George suspected, she had an illness she kept secret from all of us for months, maybe even years. All I know is that one Wednesday I had a mother who was there when I came home from school and the next Wednesday I didn't.

I walked through the ensuing days in a sort of cloud, neither believing nor disbelieving all that had happened. I'd wake up in the morning to a reality worse than any nightmare I might have had, but there was no anger. There were no screaming fits of rage, just a gray miasma that hung from above and made the world darker. I barely left the house during those first few days for fear I might see someone—one of the neighbors, the man behind the counter at the corner store—who would feel obligated to tell me how sorry they were that my mother had died. I didn't want them to see me, I didn't want them to feel sorry, I didn't want to be the boy whose mother had died. I just wanted everything to go back to the way it had been before when home, as it now seemed, was perfect.

~

After the viewings and the funeral, which took place on Thursday and Friday, the next decision that had to be made was when Benny, Thomas, and I would go back to school. Taking only the weekend and then returning on Monday, like we had all just taken a few extra days off to go down the shore, didn't seem quite right.

"When do you think the kids should go back to school?" my father and sisters conferred, while I listened in from the next room with no intention of going back anytime soon. Even though we were all Yosh and Sophie's kids, Benny, Thomas, and I were referred to both by my father and the older siblings from this point on as "the kids," a distinction that always irritated me.

"It's too soon," Donna said firmly, already taking over decisions from Yosh that my mother would have made. Then, "I think they should go back Wednesday," she said emphatically, as if that were the period of grieving that was indisputably right under the circumstances.

So Wednesday it would be. I was relieved not to have to face my peers as the motherless freak I now was for at least a few more days. I'd never seen my past self as remotely normal until I had this new identity that placed me even further outside the mainstream. So I gladly spent Monday and Tuesday in my pajamas watching game shows and soap operas, safe in the knowledge that no one would ridicule or criticize me for doing so, not even Benny. In the weeks following our mother's death, my siblings and I tiptoed around each other, with none of the teasing and sniping brothers and sisters normally do. We talked gently, quietly, as if now sharing a sixth sense. We rarely mentioned my mother after the day of the funeral, but we all seemed to understand that even the slightest raising of a voice or hint of sarcasm would be an act of unspeakable cruelty.

By Monday and Tuesday, the emptying of the house began. George, Liz, and their two little boys went back to western Pennsylvania. Larry and my sisters went back to work, with the agreement that my sisters would take turns making dinner to ensure that Yosh, Benny, Thomas, and I didn't starve to death.

Thomas was seven and a half when our mother died, and even in the depths of my own silent brooding I wondered how this blond, blue-eyed second-grader would cope with the fact that his mother was never coming back. I imagined him having a screaming fit that lasted for days. I pictured him throwing things, refusing to eat or do anything he was told, possibly even becoming unable to speak. (I knew about aphasia from watching soap operas.) Yet from what I could see, Thomas displayed absolutely no affect out of the ordinary. He played, he laughed, he said cute things that made everyone chuckle, just like before. I was nearly thirteen and felt like the ground I'd walked on for my entire life had fallen out from under me, and here was Thomas acting like nothing of any significance had happened. What had he been told, what hadn't he been told, that allowed him to just go on smiling, as if Mommy was on vacation and would be coming back in a few days? Did he even know she was dead?

Eventually, Wednesday morning came after a Tuesday night during which I had already decided I would not be going back to school, not the next day, possibly not ever. I woke up, ate breakfast, took a shower, and put on my school clothes.

~

As I entered Somerville Middle School for the first time in a week—the longest period other than school vacations I'd ever been absent—I felt on display, as if in a glass case through which no one could touch me but everyone felt compelled to look. I sensed discomfort, worry, a "there he is" look in people's eyes as I walked into the building, whether anyone in fact actually noticed me or not. Walking up to Madame Lauret's second-floor French class, which was also my homeroom, I was grateful for the school's one-way traffic flow, figuring no one could see my face if we were all walking in the same direction. But when I arrived at the classroom, I would have to look at faces, those of the kids I was in class with all day, and they would have to look at mine.

"Hi, Mike," Susie said, a little quietly and sadly, but basically the same way she said it every day.

"Hi, Suze," I said.

"Hi, Mike," Brad said.

"Hi, Brad," I said.

No one was saying or doing anything out of the ordinary. It was all just quick "Hi's" and "What's up's." Maybe this is what happens, I thought, when your mother dies and you go back to school after being absent for almost a week—nothing. Next, Madame Lauret read the announcements just like it was a regular morning, and it was all perfectly normal. At any moment, the bell would ring, and we'd move from the business of homeroom to the *bonjours* and *très biens* of French class.

Once all the announcements were read and the class was chatting and milling around the room waiting for homeroom to be officially over,

Madame Lauret walked up and leaned over my desk, her face now pale and grave.

"Michael, may I speak with you in the hall, please?" she asked in a low tone that was gentle but weighted with emotion. Now I knew this was not going to be a regular hallway conversation about making up the quizzes I'd missed. And the fact that Madame Lauret called me "Michael" in English, which she never did, made my stomach sink even lower.

I followed Madame Lauret into the dark, quiet hallway. As she stood over me, she unburdened her heavy heart: "Michael, I was just *so* sorry to hear about your mother."

Madame Lauret had known not only me but also Benny and Kathy since all of us were third-graders, when our fifteen-minute daily French classes at Van Derveer Elementary began. She seemed positively bereft by this news, at a complete loss for what to do about this terrible thing that had happened to this family with all these lovely, French-speaking children. I was not about to let myself cry in the middle of the school hallway, but Madame Lauret looked like she was about to break down herself. Then she said, shaking her head gently from side to side in desperation, "Please let me know if there's *anything* I can do. If there's *anything at all I can do* for you or your family, *please* don't hesitate to tell me. I'd like to help in *any* way I can."

An adult's response to such an expression of sympathy might be one of gratitude, felt with the full knowledge that the offer of help would never actually come to anything. But instead I was confused and started to get nervous. What did Madame Lauret mean, saying she wanted to "help in any way she can"? Was she going to just show up at our house one day? Was she going to try to cook and clean, and we'd be in such disarray as a motherless family that we wouldn't be in a position to refuse her? Suddenly, I felt mortified by the pictures forming in my mind: Madame Lauret perkily standing on our front porch while an inebriated Yosh answers the door in a dingy white undershirt and confronts her with a slurred, "Who the hell are you?" Or, Madame Lauret whipping up a quiche lorraine in our kitchen, then setting it on the table for dinner while Yosh looks visibly perplexed at the meal she's put before him.

"Thank you. I will," I simply said. Then the bell rang and the hall quickly filled with middle schoolers, thus saving me from any more discussion of this completely unthinkable scenario. I followed Madame Lauret back into the room for French class. Turning on a dime, she was back onstage.

"Bonjour, mes amis! Comment ça va?"

~

There was little more acknowledgment of my mother's death at school for the rest of the day. A few kids, mostly girls, offered quick, offhand, "Sorry to hear about your mother" condolences and then looked for other things to talk about—maybe that day's science quiz or the new song we were learning in chorus. I was grateful for the relative normalcy of it all. Then in sixth period, Miss Crosby, our English teacher, ominously asked me to step into the hallway.

"I was *so* sorry to hear about your mother," she said, using the same words and inflecting in exactly the same way Madame Lauret had that morning, as if the two of them had rehearsed it before school. By the afternoon, I was an expert at my new role—nod, say thank you, show a little sadness, then get back into the classroom as quickly as possible. My mother was dead. No conversation with a teacher was going to change that.

~

I don't remember the first afternoon I came home from school knowing my mother wouldn't be there, only flashes of what things were like in the weeks that followed. One thing I do remember is the flood of sympathy cards that filled our mailbox for weeks. Their images of flowers, or sunsets, or praying hands produced no soothing effect on me whatsoever, nor did their imprinted messages from Hallmark or American Greetings. Still, something compelled me to read them.

> At this time of great sorrow
> May you find comfort
> in the caring words of friends and family,
> And healing in the knowledge of God's love.
> With deepest sympathy.

A week or two after I'd returned to school, I found a rare piece of mail addressed to me in our mailbox. It lay buried in the stack of Hallmark envelopes and bills only my mother knew how to pay. Normally, I would have been thrilled by the novelty of getting something—anything—through the U.S. Postal Service. I was turning thirteen in a few weeks, and birthdays usually meant receiving a card from my godmother or one of my aunts with a twenty-dollar bill in it. But the return address puzzled me—it was from Todd, the boy from my lunch table who in seventh grade had stolen Sidney from me. Even though that was ancient history now, I still didn't like Todd for it, and I didn't think he particularly liked me. Why was he, of all people, sending me a letter?

Inside the envelope was a blank card with a picture of a butterfly, or a plant, or some other kind of thing a boy might be able to get away with sending to another boy, probably chosen by his mother at the pricey stationery store on Main Street. Todd wrote and wrote, filling the entire inside of the card as well as the back page with thoughts that seemed to pour out of him. I wish I still had Todd's card so that I could recall exactly what it said, but it contained lines like "I can't imagine what you must be feeling" and "I wanted to talk to you about it at school, but I just didn't know what to say." I know for sure it included this line, or a variation on it: "I didn't know your mother, but I know you, so she must have been a nice person."

He signed off the card with "Your friend, Todd." For an instant, I felt the back of my throat clench, almost as if I were going to cry.

～

Three weeks and a day after my mother's funeral was the date set for my sister Kathy's wedding. Always the family crier—set off by everything from a dog's lost tooth to a sentimental movie—Kathy could be reduced to a puddle with a single teasing word or sideward glance. All of us, Kathy included, often laughed about how easily triggered she was, but the tears she cried on the days after my mother's funeral came from a deeper place, and not only because our mother was dead.

Kathy was marrying Joe, a senior at the University of Rhode Island who had grown up in Raritan, the town next to Somerville. They had started dating when both were in high school, then Joe left for South Carolina to study biology at Clemson. But after a year of separation—and lots and lots of tears—Joe transferred to URI in order to be closer to Kathy and to start planning their wedding.

Kathy and Joe were the closest thing we had to hippies in our family—they were a free-thinking, easygoing couple, Kathy with her long, brown "Mamas and the Papas" hair and Joe with the only facial hair among any of the guys my sisters brought home. And they had a beautiful plan for their future. Joe would graduate, they would rent a little house in Narragansett, and they'd build a new, peaceful life along Rhode Island's rocky shore, close to but also far enough away from the chaos of Lincoln Avenue.

Kathy was thrown not only by my mother's death but also by the fact that she was forced to make a decision that, no matter what choice she made, was destined to make her miserable. Would she walk down the aisle with a smile on her face—and ask the rest of us to smile, too—just three weeks after our mother's body was put into the ground? Or would she put her dreams on hold for some indefinite period, waiting for a time when it would finally feel OK to be happy? And would Joe still want to get married when that time came?

"I feel bad, I feel bad," Kathy kept saying at the kitchen table, in night after night of sobbing deliberation. "I just feel so guilty," she would say, completely breaking down, Donna's and Nancy's attempts to console her producing no soothing effect at all.

Personally, I couldn't imagine going through with a wedding given everything that had just happened. Yes, more than a hundred people would have to be uninvited, everything would have to be rebooked, new dates for both the church and the VFW reception hall would have to be secured, and those would probably be months and months away. But a wedding? I had been to George's, Donna's, and Larry's weddings already, so I knew about the fancy clothes, the smiling photographs, the cocktail hour, with its hors d'oeuvres and whiskey sour fountain. Wouldn't we be betraying my mother's memory if we did all that in just a few weeks?

"I think you should go forward with it," Donna pronounced, already settling into her new role as family matriarch. "What good would it do to wait?"

Yosh, to my surprise, agreed. So we all got dressed up again—me in the already outgrown blue suit separates I'd worn to my mother's wake, Donna and Nancy in matching green bridesmaids dresses, Kathy all in white, and Yosh in a black tuxedo in which he looked uncharacteristically classy. Kathy wore a serious but tearless face down the aisle, she and Yosh did a father-of-the-bride dance to "Daddy's Little Girl," and the hired photographer snapped a family portrait with a gaping hole in it.

When we received the prints from the wedding a few weeks later, I looked through the envelope both wanting and not wanting to see this picture. Then, for months afterward, I couldn't stop looking at it. The bridal couple is smiling gamely for the camera, and Yosh has a tipsy gleam in his eye, but the rest of us look somewhere between stone faced and shell-shocked. I've often wondered, what was I trying to do, staring at this photograph over and over? Pour salt in my own wounds? Remind myself of a day when we'd all been at least a little bit happy? Accept the new reality of our lives? Maybe it was all of these or none of them. Maybe I was just trying to feel something.

9

Family Man

Yosh took some time off from work in the weeks after Sophie died and was around the house a lot—more, it seemed, than he had been for the previous thirteen years of my life combined. I'm sure he was still drinking, but he seemed reasonably sober for most of the day and tread carefully around all of us, especially Benny, Thomas, and me. No more threats to take off his belt. No more haircut rampages when he thought we looked like girls. Now my father looked at us three boys, "the kids," with a wide, frightened expression in his eyes. He was a solo parent now, and he had absolutely no idea how to be one.

He'd ask us what we wanted to eat, then realize he didn't know how to prepare it and tell one of my sisters to do it. He'd say over and over, just as he did on the day my mother died, that we would "get along," sounding more anxious and desperate whenever he faced some new task Sophie used to handle, like buying us school clothes or getting us the medicine we needed when we were sick. And when he was really grasping for ways to keep us all in one piece, whenever he saw us looking forlorn or sullen, he would promise to buy us an above-ground pool when summer came, something for which Benny and I had lobbied for years.

Yosh's sudden change in behavior left me in an emotional quandary. On the one hand, I wanted to hate my father—for all the stress he'd caused my mother over the years; for all the drinking and the tirades and the pushing and shoving that came with it; for still being alive, for being the one who survived their fight to the death; and especially for what he'd said in the driveway less than a week before she died. That refrain still haunted me, and I couldn't help wondering if my mother's death had been some form of divine punishment, brought on by my father's cavalier, hideous words.

On the other hand, did any of it matter anymore? It already seemed—and really was—a lifetime ago. The fact was that Yosh was now the only parent I had left. And he was trying to be different, trying to be a father, finally. So maybe I should try to be a son, finally?

Or were we all just being played? Was he putting on a big act hoping we'd forget about everything that had happened, hoping we'd believe he'd been a model husband and dad all along and we just hadn't noticed? The gray cloud of my mother's death hovered over me at every moment of every day, but I had no idea what or how I was supposed to feel about my father. All I knew for sure was that I really, *really* wanted an above-ground pool.

While I walked around in my state of silent ambivalence, relatively deferential to Yosh while the jury still deliberated in my head, it was pretty clear that the one in Benny's head had reached a verdict. He was fifteen, an age at which righteous anger is the default emotion for any kid, let alone one whose mother has just died and whose father had made her life miserable for the final years of her life. Benny rarely confronted Yosh directly, but whenever Yosh tried to give Benny a curfew, or advice, or an order to go grab a hammer out of the toolbox, I saw Benny's red hair get a little bit redder. I could hear his inner tirade whenever Yosh tried to act in any way parental toward him. *Who does he think he is, all of a sudden thinking he's going to be in charge?* Benny looked at my father with smoke in his eyes, slammed car doors, left the house without saying where he was going. He and I never talked about Yosh's outburst on the sidewalk the week before my mother died, but I always wondered if Benny had heard it too, and whether it factored into the balance sheet he was using to determine that Yosh, despite being our only remaining parent now, deserved nothing but his disdain.

"I'm going out!" Benny would announce after Yosh confronted him with the kinds of questions about his evening plans he'd never bothered to ask while my mother was alive. Then Benny was off, a cloud of fifteen-year-old angst trailing behind him. Not that he was going out doing anything secret or illegal—he was even more of a do-bee honor student than I was, and all of his friends were squeaky clean. But Yosh's out-of-nowhere attempts to be a dad outraged Benny, and in the privacy of our room he would say things like, "He doesn't need to know where I'm going. All of a sudden he wants to know? What the hell business is it of his?"

Trying on his new dad role, Yosh also tried to get his youngest sons to bond with him in various ways. He'd heard about an organization at the American Legion called Sons of Legionnaires and asked Benny and me if we wanted to join. I didn't know what it was or what the boys who were part of it did, and Yosh didn't seem to know either, but the mere sound of it made my skin crawl. What could possibly be going on at the American Legion that would interest Benny and me, and how in the world would we fit in with the other boys in this group? On Yosh's first attempt, I vaguely declined on behalf of myself and Benny, who wouldn't even talk about it. Undaunted by our initial rebuff, Yosh brought it up a few more times over the next few weeks, until gradually his hope turned to disappointment and then disgust with us for not playing along with his attempt at father-son socializing. I probably would have joined the group if Benny had, but he was adamant in wanting nothing to do with it.

"Sons of Legionnaires? Ugh! Is he kidding?"

Still, in the spring, Yosh made good on his promise and purchased a four-foot-deep, eighteen-foot-wide, aboveground pool. In contrast to most of the things my father brought home for us, like the secondhand organ with a few keys missing he'd acquired from "some guy at work," the pool was fresh out of the box. This was a pool the Brady Bunch could have proudly displayed in their backyard. It had a metal exterior with pastel-colored flowers all over it and a plastic liner that smelled like swimming pool heaven. I couldn't wait to unpack the box, unroll the super-mod, corrugated metal base, lay out the liner while breathing in its intoxicating vapors, snap it all together, turn on the hose, and watch it slowly fill up with summer fun.

~

An above-ground pool wasn't the only thing Yosh brought home the year after our mother died.

One morning, while I was making the coffee I had recently taken to drinking before school, Yosh told me that on Saturday night he was bringing someone to the house for Benny, Thomas, and me to meet. She was a friend he'd met a few months before, he said, and she had a daughter who was exactly my age. Maybe we'd all order pizza or get sundaes from Carvel, or both. It would be fun.

I'd heard rumblings for a while that my father might be seeing a woman. "Yosh has got a girlfriend. You mark my words!" Donna had said a few months earlier, and my other sisters seemed to believe it, too. Though Donna still called my father Daddy to his face, she was the first one to transition to referring to him as Yosh in conversations with the rest of the family. She also picked up a lot of my mother's expressions like "you mark my words," seemingly as a matter of duty, and her determination to call Yosh out whenever he tried to get away with any "bullshit."

"Donna says Daddy has a girlfriend. Do you think it's true?" I asked Benny skeptically in our room one day after school. It wasn't that I thought my father was so deeply in mourning he wouldn't be interested in another woman. I just doubted he could have found anyone willing to date him. At this point, Yosh was fifty-seven and, in my book, way over the hill in terms of being a viable boyfriend for any woman.

"I don't know. Probably," Benny tossed off with casual disdain. In his mind, Yosh was capable of anything, so whatever my sisters were saying, it was probably true. And besides, Benny couldn't have cared less what our father did. He would be off to college in two years anyway.

On the Saturday night Yosh's "friend" and her daughter were set to come over, my biggest concern wasn't whether they would measure up to my expectations but what they would think of me. This worry was heightened by the fact that something we had eaten for dinner that night had given me an intense case of flatulence. I was terrified that their first impression of me—the one who always sprayed the bathroom profusely with Glade to cover any trace I might have left behind—would be a loud, malodorous fart I'd never be able to live down.

Benny, Thomas, and I watched television in Yosh and Sophie's former bedroom, which we had redesigned with my mother's old geometric living room furniture and redubbed "the TV room," while we anticipated the big arrival. Thomas, who was eight years old now and wore his every thought and emotion on his sleeve, said things like, "What's she gonna be like?" and "I hope she's nice." Benny and I, the teenagers, sat in front of the television in cool silence.

Then the back door opened, and we all froze. A few seconds later, an unfamiliar cackle emanated from the kitchen. It was the first mature woman's laugh I'd heard in the house in a long time, possibly ever. After a minute, Yosh poked his head into the TV room, wearing the biggest smile I'd ever seen on him while sober.

"Do yous want to meet somebody?"

Peeking next through the TV room door was a dead ringer for advice columnist Ann Landers. She had a swoop of dark brown hair atop her head, which later that evening Benny said he knew was a wig: "It was obvious." The woman's hair was the color my mother's hair would have been if she'd kept up with her efforts to hide the gray. She was also about my mother's age, but she looked healthy, happy. No sunken cheeks, no deep-set frown, and she wasn't thirty pounds underweight—all the things I had grown accustomed to seeing in a fifty-year-old woman.

"I'm Elaine," she said quietly. "It's nice to meet you boys." My first impression was that she was like a middle-aged woman you might see on a TV sitcom—easygoing, pleasant, kind to children.

Then Elaine said, "This is my daughter, Claire," as a pretty teenage girl with brown hair and brown eyes shyly slunk into the room. Claire smiled vaguely but also had an "I don't want to be here" look in her eyes that said she feared it was going to be a long evening with these three boys.

"Why don't yous watch TV or play a game or something?" Yosh suggested, while he and Elaine headed back into the kitchen for an adult conversation and, no doubt, a drink.

Benny and I looked at each other in a bit of a panic, wondering how we were ever going to bring Claire out of her shell.

"Let's play Sorry!" Thomas called out right away, oblivious to the fact that Claire seemed barely able to speak, let alone play a board game. But the offer had been made, so Benny, as the oldest, felt obligated to follow through with the invitation.

"Do you want to play Sorry!?" he asked Claire. "Do you know that game?"

"I think so." Claire said timidly, barely able to get the words out. "That's the one with the sliding?"

"Yeah, it's fun!" shouted Thomas, completely forgetting as only an eight-year-old can that our games of Sorry! usually ended with his having a screaming fit and throwing game pieces across the room when he didn't win.

Colors were chosen, cards were revealed, pegs moved around the board in the quietest, most polite game of Sorry! ever to have been played at our house. There were none of the maniacal "gotchas" when someone landed on another player's piece, no meltdowns from Thomas when one of his pegs was sent back to start.

At some point in the middle of the game, despite my efforts all night to hang on, a huge grumble emerged from my intestine. Thankfully, I managed to keep it inside, but the loud "grrrrrrr" lasted for a full five seconds, sending everyone into paroxysms of laughter. I was the last to laugh, partly out of embarrassment but mostly out of fear that if I didn't hold on really tight, something even worse might happen. Eventually even I gave in, and all of us, Claire included, cracked up.

"So, do you recognize her from before?" Benny asked me after Elaine and Claire had walked out the door and Thomas was out of earshot.

"Elaine? From before what?" I asked Benny, who was now rolling his eyes like I was the biggest fool in the world.

"We met her a long time ago," he whispered scandalously. "She was the lady at the Legion. The one Daddy wanted us to meet at Kathy's shower. I guess he thinks we're stupid or something."

Benny wasn't angry or even upset. He'd liked Elaine and Claire, but true to form, he'd also figured something out.

Nearly a year and a half earlier, Benny, Thomas, and I had stopped by toward the end of Kathy's bridal shower, which took place at the American Legion hall down the street from our house. To my mother's indifferent resignation, Yosh spent most of the shower in the adjacent barroom, but when he saw the three of us had arrived, he came into the function room and insisted we follow him back to the bar. There was someone he wanted us to meet, he said. The days of my reading and math performances long gone by, I didn't like going into bars with my father anymore. I didn't like the smoke, I didn't like the sight of the shallow-eyed people on stools all obliterating themselves, I didn't like being reminded that this was my father's favorite world. But Yosh cajoled, persisted, practically dragged the three of us by our shirt collars to meet his "friend" sitting on one of the barstools, the only woman I could see in the dark, smoky room. Benny, Thomas, and I said polite hellos to her and left, completely confused about who she was or why meeting her was necessary.

Sophie had looked sideways in disgust while this whole scene unfolded, but by that point she was too exhausted to object, too spent and worn out to care. Three months later, my mother was dead.

~

Before long, Elaine and Claire became regular fixtures in our lives. Yosh and Elaine didn't get married and continued to maintain separate homes, but with our newly blended family of four school-aged children—Benny, Thomas, Claire, and me—suddenly we were all going on Saturday night outings to the movies or, better still, to my favorite place on the entire planet, the Strike and Spare Lanes. Afterward, we'd get fast food from Mr. Bee's, a kid-friendly local knockoff on McDonald's that was designed like a giant beehive, with fuzzy bumblebees covering the walls and the ceiling that you could pull off and take home. While we kids pulled bees, Yosh and Elaine would come back from the counter with the best stuff the place had to offer—milkshakes, large fries, onion rings, big premium burgers with all the toppings, not the fifty-cent stuff we used to get when my mother was alive (if we got anything at all). We would eat it right there in the restaurant or bring it back home and sit at our kitchen table, all the while laughing and telling funny stories about when each of us was little.

Soon, we started taking weeklong vacations to the Poconos in the winter and to Wildwood on the Jersey shore in the summer, a huge step up from our old day trips to the cheesy Keansburg boardwalk, where Yosh had taken us a few times when we were small.

At Keansburg, Yosh would be drunk by midday from the beer they sold at the burger stands, get tired and cranky, then demand it was time to go home just as we were starting to get lucky on the wheel of fortune or the water balloon game. After a while, my mother refused to go to Keansburg, and by the time I was in third or fourth grade, those day trips were a distant memory. By comparison, our time in Wildwood with Elaine and Claire felt like the Brady Bunch's big, three-episode trip to Hawaii. We stayed for a whole week at a motel with a built-in pool, Yosh opened his wallet for whatever we wanted, there were no major fights, and anyone passing us on the beach or at the funnel cake stand might have assumed we were just a normal family.

~

Because Yosh usually worked the 3 to 11 shift, we hardly ever saw him, Elaine, or Claire on weekday evenings. So my sisters came up with a regular schedule to make sure Benny, Thomas, and I didn't go hungry and weren't alone and unsupervised all night. My memories of these evenings are mostly stored in the part of my brain that remembers taste. I don't remember any of my sisters spending a lot of time cooking in the kitchen with my mother, but Donna must have done so before I came along, because many of her dishes were the same as Sophie's. On a Tuesday night, she might make my mother's breaded pork chops or vegetable beef soup, with a tomato base and large chunks of stew meat. Nancy, who had a full-time job and couldn't spend the afternoon in the kitchen, did most of her cooking in the crockpot, serving slow-cooked pot roast or beef stroganoff on Wednesdays. Once Kathy and Joe moved back from Rhode Island, she joined the dinner lineup on Thursdays, with chicken paprikash, cabbage and noodles, and other Hungarian dishes she had learned from Joe's mother, whom we called Recipe Rose. (If you complimented Rose on a dish she served, she couldn't resist telling you how easy it was to make. Then she would list all the ingredients and encourage you to "give it a try yourself, honey.")

But the undisputed culinary champion—to whom even my sisters willingly conceded—was bingo-playing Aunt Helen, who took Mondays in the dinner lineup. When Benny, Thomas, and I first started walking next door to Helen's on Monday nights, she tried to vary her repertoire for us—maybe fried chicken one night, my Polish grandmother's stuffed cabbage another. But once we tasted Helen's spaghetti and meatballs, there was no tasting anything else. To this day, I have never had a meatball—not in New York's Little Italy, not on Boston's North End, not anywhere—remotely approaching the flavor and texture this daughter of a Polish immigrant was able to achieve. The taste of Helen's spaghetti and meatballs dinner, which decades later lives in my sense memory in perfect vividness, is always the point of comparison when I take my first bite in any Italian restaurant. Nothing ever measures up.

"Oh my *god*, that's good!" Donna would say, tasting a spoonful from the stockpot on Helen's stove, then another. "I can see why you kids like it. Whadda you put in there?"

"I don't know!" Helen would bark, sounding frustrated by the request to explain the inexplicable but also betraying a hint of a smile, since she never received any compliments on her cooking from Uncle Ted. "I don't know what the hell I do. I just make it," she would say with a chortle, always punctuated by a Pall Mall coughing fit.

I honestly think Helen didn't know how she made her sauce, or at least she didn't think about it. Unlike my sisters, who were of a generation that used measuring cups and recipes, Aunt Helen just simmered and fussed all day Sunday, tasting and tasting until she had it right. She served her spaghetti dinner every Monday night until I graduated from high school, thus condemning me to a lifelong search for the perfect meatball.

On my sisters' nights, they would often stay around for a few hours after dinner to watch television with us or—if it was Kathy's night—play a fiercely competitive game of Sorry! or Uno. At the end of the evening, Thomas went home with whatever sister was over, then she'd bring him back to Somerville the next morning for school before she went off to work.

I often wondered what this shuttling back and forth was like for Thomas. At the time, he always struck me as the lucky one, the one everyone wanted to take home, while Benny and I stayed by ourselves until Yosh walked through the door from his late shift around midnight, by which time we were already in bed. Thomas seemed to take the whole thing in stride, happy to pack his bag and settle into one of the many bedrooms he had around Somerset County. But had Thomas ever had a chance to feel at home anywhere?

My sisters also took over holidays once my mother was gone. For Thanksgiving dinner, we started a tradition of going over to Donna and Steve's house that continued for decades. On Christmas, all three of my sisters came to Lincoln Avenue with foil-covered platters and casserole dishes, trying to re-create some of my mother's old classics: glazed ham with pineapple slices, kielbasa and pierogies, the elbow noodles with canned tomato sauce and American cheese my mother had called "baked macaroni." They brought sweaters, board games, and record albums so that we kids had presents under the tree, since Yosh's idea of appropriate Christmas gifts for children was still rain gear. It wasn't until much later in life that I realized my sisters did all this while barely adults themselves—Donna was twenty-six when my mother died, Nancy was twenty, Kathy nineteen.

~

By the time I was in high school, I finally had the one thing I'd lacked throughout elementary school—friends. Our clique, as I have to admit it was, consisted exclusively of honors-class, teacher-pleaser types, all either girls or boys who would later come out as gay men. We all liked the same things: reading books, speaking foreign languages, the challenge of taking tests and quizzes. None of them called me a fag for sharing how I felt about a book we were reading in English, or for saying "Oh, zut!" when something funny happened in French class, or for doing what teachers asked without complaint.

This group consisted of Bannister, with whom I had shared a lunch table in middle school, Sidney, on whom I still had an enormous unrequited crush, plus Amy, Cathy, Jen, Joyce, Lynn, Susie, Carrie, and—so that he wouldn't be confused with Bannister—Jimmy M. The gang.

We ate lunch together every day.

We talked on the phone constantly, sometimes to make plans for the weekend, other times just to discuss homework or, more often, the latest gossip.

At first, we spent Saturday afternoons at the roller rink or the bowling alley, dropped off and picked up by someone's parents (always theirs, not mine). Then one by one we got driver's licenses, and our supervised parent drop-offs gave way to autonomous Saturday night movies, minigolf, and skip days to the Jersey shore.

At Christmastime, we took the train into the city to see the store windows on Fifth Avenue and shop at Macy's Action Down Under, a teen-oriented department in the basement of the flagship store on 34th Street with neon lights, pulsing music, and the Jordache and Sasson designer jeans we coveted.

We celebrated one another's birthdays with all the cake, gifts, and fuss I had always wanted from my parents.

On Saturday nights, we drove to New Brunswick, where a cinema near Rutgers had midnight showings of *The Rocky Horror Picture Show*.

We wore pajamas to earn free admission, kept track of how many times each of us had seen it, and shouted all the familiar catchphrases at the screen—

> Frank N' Furter: I see you shiver with antici . . .
> Us: Say it!
> Frank N' Furter: . . . pation!

—and we never discussed the unabashedly gay content of the movie.

We lived our lives to a soundtrack of Billy Joel, Bruce Springsteen, and disco queens like Donna Summer, Gloria Gaynor, and Sister Sledge, whose big hit—"We Are Family," now a corny staple at wedding receptions—we were convinced had been written just for us. We sang that song at the top of our lungs whenever it came on one of our car radios, feeling giddily lucky to be so much more than friends.

~

I'd grown up consuming all sorts of media images of what a family was supposed to be, domestic scenes that never looked or sounded anything like the reality on Lincoln Avenue. Once my mother was dead, the TV tropes bore even less resemblance to my life, but I continued to devour them for the fantasies they allowed me to fulfill for thirty or sixty minutes every week.

In high school, my favorite show was a weekly drama simply called *Family*, which depicted the life of the WASPy Lawrences, who, in comparison to the sitcom families of my childhood and the Waltons of my middle school years, had complex, contemporary problems. The eldest daughter, Nancy, spent the whole four-year run of the series recovering from a difficult divorce; the teenage son, Willie, was a writer who had dropped out of high school and struggled to find himself; and the youngest daughter, Buddy, was an angry tomboy who often felt dismissed and unheard by the older members of the family. Yet in spite of their problems, I longed to be in a family like the Lawrences, where at the end of the day rock-solid mom and kind, patient dad were always there to pick up the pieces and say they were proud of whichever child had weathered that week's emotional storm.

I didn't understand much about family then, but I understood one thing, or at least I thought I did. Family were people from whom you had to keep certain things a secret because if you didn't, you might end up with no family at all. I could never share with anyone the guilt and self-hatred I felt about the collection of men's swimwear ads under my mattress, which had grown larger since middle school despite my daily vows to get rid of it. Nor could I talk about how every day, after a laugh-filled lunch with the gang in the cafeteria, I would take a detour down the hall toward the school's workout gym, where Jeff Bianco could almost always be found doing bicep curls on the Universal, shirtless. Standing across the hall from the gym's always-open door, I would feign a casual "I'm waiting for someone" air while furtively glancing into the gym for as long as I could get away with before I had to get to my next class. Jeff was an upperclassman with the hairy, muscled body of a twenty-five-year-old, and the fact that he never wore a shirt while working out leads me to believe that he knew his pecs, abs, and arms were worth staring at. I was obsessed with Jeff's torso. I sought it out every day and thought about it every night, doing more than just thinking while I lay in bed conjuring a picture of his perfect, perspiring body in my mind.

Nor could I talk to anyone about how, when I wasn't thinking about Jeff, I was thinking about *Family*'s Willie Lawrence, a quietly brooding, curly-haired young man with the soul of a poet who got into trouble by sleeping with too many women and never seemed to be able to make things right. I imagined comforting Willie, lying in bed next to him like one of his many girlfriends, holding him and telling him I understood him even if no one else did. I knew I couldn't feel these things for a real young man, could never allow myself to get close enough to one for it to happen. This feeling seemed entirely different and separate from the one I felt for Jeff and for the other men I was starting to notice at the beach, at construction sites, and at other places where half-naked men could be found, a feeling that simultaneously thrilled me and filled me with a shame that knew no bounds. Willie was different. Something about his story—and his curly, sand-colored hair—touched my heart. Even though he was just a TV character, Willie Lawrence was my first male crush.

When an episode aired in which Willie's best friend, Zeke, was re-vealed to be gay, I felt betrayed by Willie's initial rejection of Zeke even as I was convinced it didn't have anything to do with me. When Willie and Zeke reconciled as friends at the end of the episode, I secretly wanted them to kiss, which of course they didn't. (In those days, guest stars could be gay, but never one of a TV show's central characters.)

I didn't understand why I checked *TV Guide* every week once rerun season started to see when the Willie and Zeke episode would be re-broadcast. I didn't know why I could never bring myself to clear out the stash under my mattress or stop hanging out outside the workout gym for a glimpse of Jeff's bare torso. It never occurred to me that I could feel what I felt for Jeff and what I felt for Willie for the same person. And it certainly never occurred to me to tell anyone about what I was feeling or the things it drove me to do—not my sisters, not my brothers, not Elaine or Aunt Helen, *certainly* not my father, not even my friends, no matter how many times we sang along with "We Are Family" on our car radios. All I did was hope every night—after the dinner dishes were put away or a fun-filled evening with the gang was over—that this unspeakable part of me would disappear.

10

The Captain

Toward the end of my first year of high school, *Barron's Profiles of American Colleges* showed up at our house, a volume so hefty we could have used it as a doorstop. Benny had saved money from his afterschool job at the orthodontist's office where Nancy worked to buy the *Barron's* guide, his thousand-page roadmap away from Lincoln Avenue. Within days, the book was starred with his preliminary choices, which he had written careful notes next to like "good psychology program" and "junior year abroad." As the salutatorian of his high school class, Benny could aim high, and by the fall he whittled his initial choices down to a carefully crafted short list of what he considered his safety schools (Rutgers and Lehigh), middle-of-the-road choices (Trinity and Penn), and reaches (Brown and Stanford).

More than a few times, I flipped through the *Barron's* guide in our bedroom when Benny was out of the room, careful not to get greasy fingerprints on the pages or lose any of his bookmarks. I took in names like Swarthmore, UCLA, and Northwestern and vowed to myself that one day, one of them would redefine me.

Once the acceptance letters and financial aid offers were in and Benny made his final decision to go to Brown, he cast the book aside and it was mine. In spite of its considerable weight, holding the *Barron's* guide immediately made me feel lighter. Now it was my turn to imagine a life away from Lincoln Avenue, away from the likes of Kevin Rice and Mrs. Finch and everyone else who seemed to think it was their primary responsibility in life to knock my already questionable masculinity down a peg at every opportunity.

In high school, this job was assumed by Brian D'Aquila. Brian was the ex-boyfriend of my friend Carrie, who replaced Sidney as the girl I wanted on my arm to prove to everyone that I was a ladies' man. Carrie was, in many people's opinion, the prettiest girl in school. She had long, dark brown hair and brown eyes, and she was in all of my classes. Carrie was as uninterested as Sidney had been in a girlfriend-boyfriend relationship with me, but this time I didn't push it and just let us be two friends who happened to be a girl and a boy. Maybe the rest would just happen one day, I thought, and Carrie would realize how crazy she was about me without my having to say a word. But even if she did, I was starting to realize I might not know what to do. I didn't really know what my high school peers who were couples did with one another. Were they actually having the "sexual intercourse" we'd learned about in health class? I had no idea, and I didn't dare ask anyone about it. But whatever they were doing, I was pretty sure it went beyond the holding hands and amateur kissing of the "going with" routine of middle school.

In addition to attending the same parties, weekend movies, and summer shore outings, Carrie and I hung out together one-on-one from time to time, and this drove Brian crazy. How could Carrie want to walk down the hall between classes talking to me or do homework at her house on a Saturday afternoon with me and not with him, a star player on the football team who was better looking than I was and a lot more masculine? But academic tracking saved me again, and Brian wasn't in any classes with Carrie, our friends, and me. Still, he would find me at school and mutter "faggot" or some variation on it whenever he passed me in the hall, the cafeteria, or the parking lot. It wasn't nearly as constant as it had been with Kevin, who couldn't let five minutes go by without crawling inside my head, but in some ways it was more insidious because Brian had to go out of his way to do it. Whereas Kevin seemed to use his daily torments as a way to pass the time, all of us trapped in Mr. Farello's class all day long, Brian's pursuit of me seemed calculating, even maniacal. It made me guarded as I rounded every corner of the school, waiting for him to pop out at any moment and say:

"Faggot."

"Homo."

"Fuckin' fag."

Though this went on for two, maybe even three years, I told no one about it, least of all Carrie. Our friends group was tight—we were family, after all—but no one ever said anything remotely related to being gay. (It would be years, well beyond high school, before those floodgates would open.) And it was all cutting a little too close to the bone now, given all the male fantasies and swimwear porn I was keeping secret. So when Brian would swing by and drop one of his f-bombs on me, I would flash for a moment back to sixth grade, when Kevin had made me his emotional punching bag. For five minutes, or sometimes for the rest of the day, I'd feel the familiar sensation of being attacked, humiliated, and also somehow at fault. Then I'd just go to my next period and chat with Carrie, Susie, Bannister, and everybody else until the bell rang, as if nothing had ever happened.

But Brian also played a useful role in my high school career by adding himself to the growing roster of people to whom I had something to prove. Now that I had a year-old *Barron's* guide in my hands, I was going to plot my own route out of Somerville and toward a future that would not only surprise all of them but make them deeply, insanely jealous. Like a sudden flash of lightning, I saw the word "theatre" on the list of majors at the front of the *Barron's* book, and a forward path cleared right before my eyes: I was going to become a famous actor. I would have it all: fame, money, a TV show (my life would become a sitcom after all), looks, an apartment in New York, a house in Hollywood. I would walk into restaurants and get the best table without a reservation. I would become special in everyone's eyes again, and Sheila, Kevin, Mrs. Finch, Brian, and all of their kind would grovel for one-minute "remember when" conversations with me, which I would refuse to grant. It was the perfect solution, the only ending to my story that made any sense. Why hadn't I thought of it before?

In addition to my detailed knowledge of just about every television show that had ever aired from the late 1960s onward, I had an acting résumé that stretched all the way back to first grade, when I'd played the lead role in *Too Much Noise!* While the other kids were assigned to play animals who mooed and neighed and created a general racket, I was cast as ornery protagonist Peter, the farmer who was determined to stop the noise and have a quiet barnyard. By all accounts, it was a tour de force. *Too Much Noise!* was followed up by a production in third grade in which I played a sea captain and a mystery in eighth grade in which I played Wentworth, the butler, who was presumed dead but made a surprise appearance during the final scene of *The Phantom Strikes Again*.

In high school, my acting career hit a dry spell when the only performance opportunities available to freshmen, sophomores, and juniors were in the spring musicals. I was then, and remain to this day, a klutz on my feet, and Bannister's superior dance skills always landed him the lead roles. So I ended up in the choruses of *Annie Get Your Gun, Damn Yankees*, and *Bye-Bye Birdie*. I already viewed the chorus as an unglamorous assignment—would anyone notice or care how I delivered my one line ("Look! Over there!") in the middle of a big group number? Then one morning I found myself in an unplanned conversation with Yosh while getting ready for school.

"Are ya gonna go out for football?" he asked, completely out of the blue, while I poured myself a cup from the Mr. Coffee. By this point, Yosh's urgings for me to get involved in athletics were taking on an anxious, almost panicked tone, as if my future were a moving train and he was desperate to get me to switch tracks before I ended up at the wrong destination.

"Football's over," I said with a groan.

"Then you should go out for baseball," he reasoned, as if playing varsity in either sport required no prior experience or special skill.

"I can't do baseball. I'm in the play," I said.

Now I was dipping my toe into uncharted waters. Generally, I kept my interest in theatre from my father. It wasn't worth getting into, because I knew he wouldn't get it at all. But maybe I could use it to explain, once and for all, why I didn't have time for sports.

"You're in the play? What play?"

"*Annie Get Your Gun*."

Silence.

"It's a musical."

"Well, what do you play? What kind of a part?" Yosh asked, now showing a tiny spark of interest. I guess watching his old westerns on TV gave him some frame of reference for the world of acting.

"I'm in the chorus," I said.

"The what? Whuzzat mean?"

"I sing some of the songs and do some of the dances."

"But what *part* do you play?"

"It's a lot of different parts," I said, by now walking out of the kitchen, sans coffee, just looking for a way out.

"So, what are you, just one of the crowd?"

Silence.

"Anybody can do that," he shouted up the stairs to which I had already retreated, attempting to impress on me a point he found perfectly logical. "I don't know why you waste your time on that. You should go out for football."

∼

During senior year, there were two opportunities to be cast in productions at the high school, the spring musical and the senior class play, which took place in the fall. For the musicals Ms. Greer, the theatre director, never quite knew what to do with me as a tall, awkward kid who could sing reasonably well but couldn't dance a step. But I had paid my dues as a dedicated member of the drama club for three years, and in the spring of my junior year Ms. Greer said she was looking out for me. She'd chosen a senior class play with a great role for me in mind.

That September, I was cast as Captain Keller, Helen Keller's father, in *The Miracle Worker.* As depicted in the play, Keller was a booming tyrant who fought the efforts of Annie Sullivan to teach Helen how to use language and dismissed them as a futile waste of time. He ran his household the way he had run his army battalion. He was forceful, in charge, accustomed to being obeyed. This did not come naturally to me, the kid who always apologized just for being in the room. About halfway through the rehearsal process, Ms. Greer seemed at a loss for how she could turn a sixteen-year-old whose body language said "I know, I know, I'm a fag" into Captain Keller. She had an entire cast and crew to worry about.

But my friend Amy, who was assistant director of the play and had all the bossiness required to be a good one, was not about to let me off easily. Every time I went backstage after a limply executed scene, thinking I would just gossip with the rest of the cast until my next entrance, Amy would drag me aside and tell me we were going to work on Keller.

"You're the captain! You're in charge! Stand up straight! Let me see you walk. No! Straighter! Take charge!"

But I didn't feel like a captain, didn't have a clue what that could possibly mean. I didn't feel like a man, or even a boy—how could I feel like a captain? At this point I just wanted to quit the play and go home, sensing it was all headed for one big, embarrassing flop. Maybe Amy should play Captain Keller, I thought. *She* knew how to be a tyrant. But Amy wasn't about to give up on me, and one day—just to shut her up—I gave her what she asked for: a straight spine, which led to a laser-focused gaze ahead, which could only be accompanied by a voice that issued commands instead of apologies. And in the wings of the Somerville High School auditorium, Captain Keller started to come to life.

From that afternoon on, when I strode up and down the platforms and walked through the door frames that the Somerville High set crew had made to depict the Keller home, it was my kingdom. Sitting at the head of the dining room table, I commanded my wife, Kate, my son, James, and that presumptuous "cub of a girl" Annie Sullivan to do as I said, and they quietly deferred. "Yes, Captain," they said to my every order. Every day at rehearsal, I ruled the Keller house. And soon I'd rule an audience, too.

On opening night, I looked in the mirror and, for the first time, saw the captain from the outside: the austere, dark gray suit separates pulled by the theatre moms from the costume storage rack; the finely trimmed beard held on by spirit gum and grayed with Ben Nye white by the makeup crew to match my salted-and-peppered hair; the wire-rimmed reading glasses I would use to write a letter to a doctor who might be able to help my poor, "afflicted" daughter.

Was I nervous about the fact that an audience was going to be filling the seats that had been empty during months of rehearsals? Was I terrified that for the first time in my life, there would be a Sadowski contingent at one of my performances? No one had ever come to any of my previous plays or choral concerts before, not even my mother. So having Yosh, Aunt Helen, and my sisters out there might have led me to panic. But I knew I was damn good in this role. All I had to do was go out there and show them.

~

When the curtain went up on *The Miracle Worker*, I had command of the Keller household just as I'd had in rehearsals. I thought I had command of the audience, too, but it was hard to know for sure. Then we got to the showdown.

In one of the play's final scenes, Captain Keller challenges Annie Sullivan about the way she is teaching Helen, and his son stands up to him, presumably for the first time in his life.

"She's right!" young James Keller says to his father emphatically, with a boldness that surprises even himself. "Kate's right, I'm right, and you're wrong! . . . Has it never occurred to you that on one occasion you might be consummately *wrong*?"

Silence falls over the audience. Then, after a few seconds, it is broken by a woman in the front row, who lets out a low, slow sound of genuine horror.

"Ughhhhhhhh!!!" she moans, as if a shocking development has just rocked the town where one of her afternoon soap operas takes place. It is Aunt Helen. The sound she makes is involuntary. She is completely wrapped up in the story.

Another silence, then—a burst of applause. To the audience's great satisfaction, someone has finally stood up to the tyrannical Captain Keller. And Michael Sadowski is not even in the room.

~

"Ohmigod! You were *so* good!"

"You were *amazing*!"

The chorus of praise from friends and acquaintances got me high on a drug to which I was now completely addicted. When I found the family in the lobby, my sisters expressed genuine surprise at my performance, and Aunt Helen still seemed a little shaken by the unexpected plot twist at the end of the play. Finally, Yosh weighed in.

"You played a real good part," he said quietly, shaking his head and looking down a little. There wasn't even a hint of a smile on his face— just genuine awe. Who *is* this teenage boy he thought he knew? I'd grown a few inches that year, especially with the arrow-straight spine and confident bearing Amy had drilled into me. And there, in the lobby of my high school auditorium, I noticed—for the first time, as I remember it—that I was taller than my father.

The next day at breakfast, Yosh shook his head, looked down in the same awestruck, almost somber way, and quietly said the same words:

"You played a real good part." It became his new refrain for the next few weeks. My father had always been sparing in his praise, but when he latched onto the idea that one of his children had done something remarkable, he talked about it to anyone who would listen. Not since our barroom and pigeon club days, when I read headlines from the newspaper to win him free drinks or he passed around my report card to show his buddies, had I been the subject of his boasting.

~

During my last two years of high school I was, in every practical sense, an only child. The house that had once been raucous with my parents' shouting matches and the bickering of eight brothers and sisters all vying for one bathroom was now down to just my father and me.

Thomas was out of the house now, having gone to live with Donna and Steve who decided, with little objection from Yosh, that my younger brother needed a more stable and consistent home life. Yosh still mostly worked the afternoon shift at the paint factory, so I usually only saw him in the early mornings before school. After having been on the wagon for a while, he was drinking a lot again, now Fleischmann's rye whiskey mixed with ginger ale, his highballs as he called them. He drank more quietly and privately now to keep it from Elaine, who broke up with him on and off when he got out of control, then took him back on and off when he promised to straighten up and fly right. Before school, I would come downstairs to make my coffee and lightly buttered toast—the breakfast of choice for the weight-conscious aspiring actor I now was—and Yosh would be staring out the window, half-reading the *Daily News* and concealing a 7 a.m. highball under the kitchen table. Most days, we didn't say two words to one another, but about once a week he would ask:

"You need money?"

If a school trip was coming up or if it was Friday and my friends were going out to a movie, I might say yes, taking the ten or twenty he pulled from his wallet, which always came with the admonition, "Don't spend it all in one place." But most of the time I said no, using my refusal as a perverse kind of payback for something. His drinking? My mother? All the times he'd told me I should go out for football? I don't know. Then I would leave for school and not be aware of his existence again until I heard him pull into the driveway after the late shift, close to midnight, just as I was falling asleep.

Benny was also gone from the house now, having left for college: Brown for a year, followed by a transfer to Columbia, the circumstances of which it would take me years to piece together.

The first clue was a letter I found in the bedroom Benny occupied while he was home for the summer after his first year at Brown. My heart beat faster as I stared at it on top of his dresser. I knew I shouldn't be in his room. I knew I shouldn't be thinking about looking at a letter addressed to him. But it was *right there*, slit open at the top, and it called to me with the sexy intrigue of its beautiful handwriting, which spelled out "Ben Sadowski" and our address in fancy black fountain pen. From the return address—Keeler, New York, NY—I knew it was from Grayson, a friend of Benny's I'd met when I'd visited him at Brown earlier that year.

I liked Grayson. He was, according to the "who's who" breakdown Benny gave me before I spent the night at the dorm, a blueblood from Manhattan whose family also had a house on Nantucket, a place unimaginable from the vantage point of Lincoln Avenue. I caught no hint of looking-down-his-nose snobbery when I met Grayson, though. He had a patrician air about him, for sure, but he was kind and pleasant looking, if unremarkably handsome. The weekend I was at Brown, Grayson went a little out of his way to find out what made "Ben's brother" tick. By this point, I knew I was going to be an actor, and I used this fact to position myself as artsy and intriguing among Benny's hard-to-impress college friends, especially Grayson, who seemed at least mildly interested in my theatrical aspirations.

I had my first experience with marijuana on that visit, high on brownies under the gaze of a group of college first-years, who I'm sure were highly entertained watching their friend's fifteen-year-old, green-as-grass brother get stoned. I was disappointed that Grayson wasn't around the night of the pot brownies, and I asked Benny if he was going to be there because I liked the way he smiled at me, the attention he threw my way. I wanted him to see me fit right in with the rest of the college gang, to see how cool and sophisticated I was.

"No, Grayson isn't really part of the main crowd here," Benny explained, a little dismissively. "We're friends, but he doesn't really fit in with Jake and Don and the others that much. He kind of does his own thing most of the time."

As if by some uncontrollable impulse, I pulled the letter out of the envelope and unfolded it. Immediately, lines beautifully penned on Grayson's high-quality stationery jumped off the page.

I really miss you.

It would be wonderful if you could come to Nantucket and visit this summer. I'd love to see you.

I can't stop thinking about you and what we had.

By now, I could feel my heartbeat pounding in my chest, thumping in my neck, and pulsing in my temples all at the same time. This was the first time in my life I had ever heard a man say such things to another man—and the person on the receiving end of these words was *my brother.* Even as naïve as I was at fifteen, it was obvious to me from the letter that Grayson was gay and very possibly that Benny was, too. At the very least, Grayson and Benny had "had" something, something Benny was ending by not returning to Brown—and Grayson was desperate to it get back.

My first impulse was to feel sad for Grayson, not only because he was gay—which I thought was definitely a reason to feel sorry for someone—but because he was a nice guy and was obviously in love with my red-headed brother, who had a knack for attracting people he didn't love back. In high school, they were usually girls, but now that Benny was in college and was smoking weed and doing other things I'd never known him to do before, anything seemed possible.

I love you, and I know you loved me. Or at least I thought you did.

My mind still spinning to figure out what it all meant, as if I didn't already know, I looked over my shoulder repeatedly to make sure I didn't see Benny coming up the stairs, then carefully placed the letter back in the envelope. I tried my best to remember how the pages I'd rifled through had been oriented and at exactly what angle the letter had been sitting on the dresser. Benny was smart—he noticed things—and I had to get it just right.

Once I was safely out of the room, I went next door to my own room, sat on my bed, and sighed with relief that I hadn't been decapitated yet. Then my mind turned to wondering what I was going to do with my new knowledge—Benny, Grayson, the letter, "I love you," all of it. After a few minutes, the answer emerged with perfect clarity: nothing. I obviously couldn't talk to Benny about it. The content alone made that impossible, not to mention the fact that I would have to confess to having read a letter addressed to him, an offense for which he might justifiably have killed me. And if we started to talk about Grayson and "what they had," what else would we end up talking about? Why did I want to know, he'd ask. Why the hell did I care so much? So I simply filed away the information, just as I had filed away so many things before, in a locked drawer somewhere inside me.

Still, I felt that letter's presence at every moment from then on. Suddenly, in the middle of a dull summer afternoon on Lincoln Avenue, a romance between two men had come right into our house. It hung in the air in the room next to mine and stayed there even after Benny moved out to go to Columbia. Gayness, once only the subject of gossip among my friends and a very small number of ahead-of-their-time TV episodes I had watched, now defined my brother to me. And this forced me to define myself, too.

My logic—if a state of denial one only half believes can be called that—went something like this: If Benny was gay, then I couldn't be. First of all, lightning wouldn't strike the same house twice, would it? Second, it had been clear from the start that Benny and I were different. With him, at least in hindsight, all the signs had always been there—his playing with dolls in early childhood; the meticulous way he cleaned the pool and our room; the fact that all of his friends were girls, instead of just most of them, like mine. He was gay and I was an actor. Actors were not gay. Actors were leading men, romantic heroes, heartthrobs on soap operas. Of all the actors I knew about from television and movies, I'd never heard of a single one being gay. It just wasn't possible.

~

The Miracle Worker was in November of my senior year, close to Thanksgiving. This meant that when it was over it was time to return to the hand-me-down *Barron's* book and make my final selections. With the exception of NYU, which required an audition that I could get to on my own via commuter train and subway, I hadn't visited any of the colleges on my short list. Yosh was hardly the college-visit type, so sight unseen, and following Benny's formula, I sent off six applications to schools based on little more than catalog descriptions.

Stanford appealed because it was elusive and would give me bragging rights within the family—it had been the only school that rejected high-flying Benny. It also was located in the glamorous, exotic, unseen land of California, three thousand miles away from Lincoln Avenue. Then there were Cornell and the University of Pennsylvania, two Ivies that seemed within my academic reach, and Northwestern in the same general category of competitiveness, which also had a first-rate theatre program and lots of famous alums in the entertainment industry. NYU and Rutgers were too close to home to really have a chance, though the prospect of hanging around Washington Square, then swinging a dance bag over my shoulder and hopping on the subway for auditions uptown had a certain appeal.

First came a response from Rutgers's Cook College, the liberal arts division to which I had applied, with no attempt to excite me with gushy language. Its Courier font form letter read something like this.

The admissions committee has reached the following decision with re-gard to your application.
　　Cook College: Admit

I don't remember what order the rest came in, but Stanford told another Sadowski to stay back east. I got into NYU, despite an audition for which I was ridiculously underprepared, and into Penn, but it also was too close to home and in Philadelphia, which didn't even have the bohemian appeal of Greenwich Village going for it. So it was down to Cornell and Northwestern, both of which sent letters that started like this:
　　We are pleased to inform you . . .
Both financial aid packages were generous. It would cost me a now-unfathomable eighteen hundred dollars a year to attend either school, room and board included, and I could cover the shortfall with small loans and with the Social Security checks I received as a surviving de-pendent of my mother. Since the two universities were nothing more than names to Yosh and I didn't see much of Benny anymore, I was left pretty much on my own to make the decision. Ms. Greer, who had majored in theatre and had married an unemployed filmmaker, was one of the few people in my circle to express an opinion about my options. She had a practical sense about the prospects of a successful career in the arts and thought I should choose Cornell and major in English. If you got into an Ivy League school and could afford it, she thought, you

should go—case closed. But the notion of a sprawling rural campus in upstate New York, bucolic and beautiful as it was reported to have been, was no match for the lure of Northwestern's high-powered theatre program just outside Chicago, which might as well have been Paris for what it represented to a Jersey kid who had never set foot outside the eastern time zone.

~

To this day, whenever I fly, I love the sensation of takeoff. I stop doing whatever I'm doing or put down whatever I'm reading to take it in: the rumble that surrounds you as you taxi on the runway; the rolling motion that gets faster and faster until the plane can no longer remain parallel to the ground; the ascent that forces you back into your seat, helpless against gravity; then the leveling, which quiets the cabin into a low, white noise and settles you into airspace, where all you can do is surrender to the promise of your destination.

At the age of seventeen, I took my first flight. For seventy-nine dollars I traveled one way on Allegheny Airlines, which was later to become US Airways, from Newark to Chicago, from Lincoln Avenue to the life I had chosen for myself. On a sunny September morning, Yosh dropped me off curbside at Newark Airport with a duffel bag the size of a five-year-old and one piece of advice he issued in a finger-wagging tone.

"Now, keep your nose clean!" he said, his voice breaking a little. Then he immediately looked down and away from me.

"I will," I said, assuming it was what I was supposed to say in response to this old-fashioned maxim I didn't understand, and closed the trunk of the car decisively.

Then Yosh was off to the rest of his day, the rest of his life, and so was I. I checked in, went through security, boarded, and took off. In the air, I never once thought about home. What was left of home anyway? And had anything ever happened there that I would want to remember?

11

Big Man on Campus

What'syournamewhat'syourmajorwhereyoufrom?

Within minutes of finding the Wildcat Welcome crew, a cheery group of fresh-faced upperclassmen stationed at O'Hare Airport to pick up new arrivals, I learned that this three-part question was the mantra of New Student Week at Northwestern. "MichaelSadowskitheatreNewJersey," I answered over and over, proudly declaring my new star-in-the-making identity as I circulated among the twenty or so students who were gathered at baggage claim to take the bus to campus.

To my surprise, no one else in this group was majoring in theatre, nor was anyone else getting dropped off at my dorm, Sargent Hall. Given Northwestern's size, I figured these weren't students I was going to be seeing much of once we arrived on campus, so I didn't put in any special effort to make friends. All of them also had parents in tow who had come to help them get settled in, so while the families clustered and chatted in the front and middle of the bus, I headed for a solo seat toward the back and stared out the window as we pulled away from O'Hare. Why talk to someone's mother and father, whom I would probably never see again, when all around me was Chicago, an exciting city I'd heard about all my life?

For most of the bus trip, Chicago was just an interstate with a bunch of airport hotels and low-rise corporate buildings that looked only slightly less gritty than the New Jersey highwayscapes I was used to. But I didn't care—it was all new. We passed signs for avenues I'd never heard of: Cumberland, Montrose, Cicero. The interstate signs looked more or less like the ones back home, except instead of "New Jersey" they said

"Illinois" in tiny letters above the number 90, and then 94 as we headed toward the North Shore. I set my Timex back an hour and tingled with the realization that I now lived somewhere far, far away from Lincoln Avenue.

Sargent Hall was an unremarkable brick building the color of wet sand. It looked like a small high school, its L-shape, metal doors, and straight lines suggesting "government-funded building" rather than the Gothic-style, ivy-covered student sanctuary I'd been expecting. Heading upstairs toward my assigned room on the fourth floor, I was surprised to find the dormitory's orange plaster halls mostly empty, the buzz of meeting and greeting I'd anticipated having not yet materialized. Clearly, I was one of the earliest arrivals or everyone was out touring campus with their parents, I wasn't sure which. I did find Rich, the resident assistant, a stocky midwesterner who gave me my keys, plus the obligatory cheery handshake and name/major/state exchange.

The room underwhelmed me with its built-in, symmetrical arrangement of curved desks and connected single beds, which were in an outdated blond wood grain reminiscent of a set of bilevel end tables my mother had thrown out years before. But the aesthetics of the dorm didn't matter much to me anyway. The real draw of Sargent—the reason I had chosen it—was the lakefront that, according to the campus map provided in the prospective student catalog, lay directly behind it. So instead of setting up house right away—and possibly offending my new roommate by taking the side of the room he wanted—I set down my fifty-pound duffel dead center and headed out Sargent's back door to find the real Northwestern, the one I'd seen in all the photographs.

Behind the dorm, just as the campus map had promised, was North Campus beach and, beyond that, Lake Michigan. As far as the lakefront was concerned, Northwestern lived up to all the pictures in the brochure. The lakefill, as it was called because it was built on land that had been filled in over what had previously been part of Lake Michigan, was a long expanse of green grass with a paved jogging and biking trail that ran along a rocky shore. It reminded me of the rocks of Narragansett Beach, which I had seen when Kathy and Joe lived in Rhode Island, and the lake might as well have been the Atlantic Ocean at low tide, because looking east, gently rolling waves were all you could see. To the south, just as the catalog pictures had shown, was the Chicago skyline, a reminder on this peaceful, resort-like lakefront that Northwestern offered the best of both worlds. Urban sophistication and excitement were just an El ride away. But "the rocks," as I learned they were called, the boulders that lined the lakeshore, were what excited me the most. Here I would choose my special promontory, sit, and stare out at the endless lake. I would contemplate the big questions of life and rehearse the Shakespeare monologues that would make me a great tragedian. And, when I had a girlfriend, we would sit on a special rock we had chosen just for us, hold hands, and gaze at the lapping water while we envisioned our future.

"SheriMoskowitztheatreNewYork" and "DavidSarantinotheatreNew-Jersey" were the first two students I met upon my arrival back on North Campus. They were standing in the mailroom and were already in theatrically animated midconversation when I arrived. Sheri and David seemed as happy as I was to have met kindred spirits, ports in the storm of first-day newness and strangeness. I laughed for the first time since I'd arrived, since it struck us all as ironic that we'd come all the way to Evanston, Illinois, only to meet our first theatre peers from the tristate area.

"Let's go to Norris later," we said, as we made a vague plan to get together at the student center that afternoon for coffee, ice cream, book shopping, who remembers what. No doubt, it was one of hundreds of quicky kinships that were forming all over campus that day, some of which would evolve into actual friendships, but most of which wouldn't.

Sargent was a coed dorm, but it was sex-segregated by floor, and by the time I got back from my walk along the rocks the fourth-floor guys were in full attendance: Jim from Georgia, Ed from Kansas, Pete from California, Jake from Oklahoma. They were universally friendly and welcoming—not a hint of anyone saying or even thinking I was a fag. My roommate, Darren, was also there when I returned. A gangly kid with a thick Midwest accent, oversized clothes, and a mop of jet-black hair, Darren gave me a huge smile and a floppy handshake. Right away, I could tell Darren liked to laugh, and it wasn't long before I also learned he had a penchant for practical jokes. Soon after we moved in, he took to throwing water balloons out of the fourth-floor window into the alley while unsuspecting "tech weens"—the engineering nerds Darren considered especially hilarious targets, despite the fact that he was an engineering major himself—exited the technology building next door. Though

Darren was clearly the ringleader, other guys from the fourth floor joined in the water balloon bombings from time to time, cheering and chortling while their victims searched the heavens for the source of their dousing. I was starting to get the sense that the fourth-floor guys were not going to be the sophisticates I'd expected to be having deep, late-night conversations with at the University of My Mind.

If the fourth-floor guys lacked the maturity and sophistication I was looking for in college life, the theatre students I met at Northwestern, at least to my seventeen-year-old mind, had an overabundance of it. Sargent, as a north campus dormitory, was filled with students from the science and technology fields whose department buildings dominated that part of campus. But in a social experiment of sorts, a cluster of first-year and a few sophomore and junior theatre students were also placed there, almost exclusively on the second and third floors. These students were witty, well read, and well traveled, deeply knowledgeable about classical music and Renaissance art and a lot of other things to which I'd had no exposure. And some were very, very rich. Certainly some had gone to public schools, but an equal number—as their freshman pic book profiles indicated—went to schools with names like Phillips Exeter Academy, the Dalton School, and Choate that so obviously signaled wealth and privilege, I didn't have to look them up to find out. For the first time, a keen awareness of social class crept into my being. After what I perceived as a few haughty looks from kids whose parents were full payers, I learned not to talk about financial aid, not to tell everyone that I was at Northwestern on a generous package that allowed me to attend for less than two thousand a year, room and board included. I learned not to tell old Somerville High stories but to emphasize instead that I had "gone to Montserrat," a tiny music school with a fancy name near our house where I had once taken a few voice lessons. (Therefore, this was technically true.) I learned to say my father was a "plant supervisor," not a factory worker and pigeon racer, and never, ever to talk about his drinking, something I didn't realize rich parents did as much of as my own father.

The proximity that most of the cluster members had to one another on the second and third floors meant that they were in and out of each other's rooms all the time. Unlike the testosterone-driven fourth floor, it was guys and girls together, no doubt having the kinds of long, philosophical conversations I longed for at all unpredictable hours of the day and night. Technically, I was part of the cluster—I sat at the cluster table during dinners with our advisor—but visiting their space in the dorm always felt like just that: visiting, invading their territory, putting a kink in a day-to-day rhythm that was already well established.

One exception to the theatre cluster clannishness was Howard, a junior, who seemed to like hanging out with freshmen he could make laugh. Howard was an aspiring comedian with a rambling, Woody Allen–like schtick. His always-running commentary included calling anyone in the dorm or theatre program whose behavior he found offensive a "major fuckhead." He appreciated my enjoyment of his sardonic stand-up routine and took me under his wing during my first week at the dorm. In one of our conversations, I mentioned to Howard that I was a singer. He quickly grabbed me by the shoulder and launched into a monologue.

"Hey! You should check out these auditions my friend Jason just told me about," he said. The auditions were for a musical revue called *This Time It's the Big Time*, a student-concocted revue of songs from 1970s Broadway musicals. "This guy Bill got a Broadway gig over the summer. Tough break, right? But they have to replace him, and they want to see freshmen because they've already auditioned everybody else. He was supposed to sing a duet with Colette. Have you met Colette? You know who Colette is, right?"

I shook my head, because I hadn't met or heard of any Colettes on campus.

"Ohmigod. Colette is only, like, the most beautiful girl on the entire campus, and she has the voice of a goddess. Ohmigod! Can you imagine if you could do a song with her?" He grabbed my shoulder again, a little tighter this time. "You *have* to go to this audition, my friend! *Check it out!*"

⁓

When I walked into the audition room, there they all were: about a half-dozen cast members who looked like they had just stepped out of the TV commercial for *A Chorus Line*. To my thoroughly green eyes, this was, in fact, the "big time." I met Howard's friend Jason, whose leg warmers and tights immediately marked him as a serious dancer, and the director, Clark, who was probably only a couple of years older than me but who might as well have been in his forties for the directorial air he projected from behind the audition table. And standing by the piano in the corner, going over a piece of sheet music with the musical director between auditions, was—undoubtedly—Colette, the most beautiful young woman I'd ever seen in my life. She had brown hair, brown eyes, and a smile that illuminated her entire face. And the notes I heard coming from the corner of the room were, as Howard had promised, pure magic.

I sang "On the Street Where You Live," the only musical theatre song to which I could find the sheet music on short notice, and was reasonably happy with the result. I remembered all the lyrics, and the high note was there when I needed it. Then I learned a dance combination that, though mercifully simple, still took me multiple corrections to perform. Clark said they would post the cast list the following day, which surprised me because even the auditions for our high school musicals went on for a full week. But the show was just three weeks away, and rehearsals were starting the next evening. There was no time to waste.

Later that night I got back to the dorm and checked in with Howard, who I figured would be dying to know how the audition had gone. As I rounded the corner toward Howard's room I saw that the door was open and, before I could get away, there was Jason, the dancer from *Big Time*, sitting on Howard's bed. They both looked at me wide eyed, and then at one another nervously for a minute, unsure of what to say or do.

Finally, apparently concluding there was no reason to hold back, Jason said, "Congratulations."

I froze in place, not willing to let myself believe it yet.

"Wow! Really?" I said, while Howard glowed, his protégé having scored a duet with the legendary Colette. "I thought I kind of screwed up the dance part."

"Well, yeah, we'll work on that." Jason said with a bit of a shrug. "But everybody thought you sounded great. And, to be honest, you were the best-looking guy there. And let's face it, you can't just stick anybody with Colette."

This was the best possible news of all. Singing: 10. Looks: 10 (or at least 6). Dance: 3, but "we'll work on that." I was on my way. Classes hadn't even started and I had landed a plum role during my first week on campus. Immediately, I played up my status as working actor among my peers, whose days were still filled with the mixers and orientation meetings of New Student Week. Halfway through dinner with the theatre cluster, I'd sling my large duffle bag, now filled with the jazz shoes, leotard, and tights I'd purchased at the dance supply store downtown, over my shoulder. Offhandedly, I'd announce before the others had even gotten back in line for dessert, "I have to go. I have rehearsal."

~

"Five, six, seven, eight!" Clark yelled out, sounding like Bob Fosse during rehearsals for our group dance numbers. Then, just as predictably, "Mike, relax your shoulders!"

Despite my attempts to replicate the fluid jazz moves that were the hallmark of the 1970s Broadway shows we were honoring in *Big Time*, my body was tight—really tight, holding on to things that it would still take me years to figure out were there. The three weeks of dance drills and constant reminders to relax my shoulders helped a little, and I got through the dance numbers without any major flubs, but I know I looked stiff onstage.

I don't remember much from the opening night performance or any subsequent ones, just isolated images: the multicolored footlights that were more dazzling than anything we'd had in high school; the black leotards and tights that were the cast uniform and that, with the bit of extra weight I've always carried around the middle, made me look a little like a sausage; the kick line we did during the title number that made me feel like I really was in *A Chorus Line*. (As I learned doing *Big Time*, kick lines always draw applause from the audience, even though they're the easiest of all dance moves to perform.) I remember stepping into the light with Colette for our big duet, "Too Many Mornings" from Stephen Sondheim's *Follies*, which was *Big Time*'s eleven o'clock number, right before the finale.

The Sargent theatre cluster came to see *Big Time* on the second night, and I was thrilled at the prospect of showing them all that, whatever my peripheral social placement, I was a special member of the group. They told me the show was great, went on and on about the stuff one is supposed to go on and on about after seeing a peer in an amateur show. Who knows what anyone really thinks in such situations? All I know for sure is that after that, life in the dorm pretty much went on as before— the cluster members moving in and out of one another's rooms, always seeming to be in midconversation when I arrived.

~

One day before a *Big Time* rehearsal, Colette asked if I was planning to join a fraternity, and I had never remotely considered the possibility. I knew Northwestern was one-third Greek, but I had always assumed that, based on my long-standing aversion to any kind of settings where male bonding took place, I would be part of the two-thirds majority that stayed away from the frats. My image of fraternities up to that point was limited to the movie *Animal House*, and I'd already had a taste of immature frat boy behavior on the fourth floor. But Colette said that Phi Psi, her boyfriend's fraternity, was nothing like that. She was there all the time, and they were nice, serious, mature guys. I should go to one of their parties during rush week, tell them she'd sent me. The idea of living in a house completely occupied by men terrified me, and I was still pretty skeptical about whether this kind of scene could possibly be for me. But Colette was in a sorority herself and seemed to know what she was talking about—after all, she was *Colette*.

The Phi Psi house, as it turned out, was right next door to Sargent, so I could stop in on my way home and, if it was the waste of time I expected it to be, still be in my dorm room five minutes later. With Colette's endorsement in my back pocket, I walked into the Phi Psi living room and immediately took in the scene: casually well-groomed guys in top siders, worn sockless, and Lacoste alligator polos or slightly wrinkled oxford shirts with the tails hanging out over knee-length shorts or khakis. Never one for introducing myself in unfamiliar situations, I scanned the room immediately for someone I knew. I couldn't find Colette anywhere.

Just as I was about to head back to my dorm and give up on this crazy fraternity idea, a handsome upperclassman walked up to me and held out his hand. Based on his comfortable, regal tone—the air of owning the place that he projected—I knew right away he was a member.

"Hi, I'm Kyle. Nice to meet you."

"MichaelSadowskitheatreNewJersey," I answered before he even had a chance to ask. I talked about being in the show, singing with Colette and knowing her boyfriend (sort of), and living next door in Sargent. I was completely unaccustomed to this kind of positive attention from a handsome, expensively dressed young man, and my head tingled. I was feeling both flattered and smitten, though I only acknowledged one of these emotions at the time. This being the early part of rush week,

Kyle moved on pretty quickly to other conversations—his job was obviously to welcome all the freshmen in the room and quickly check them out as potential pledges. A few more members approached me in a similar way, and we repeated the instinctual mating ritual that was fraternity rush—them the solicitous hosts, me the prospective new pledge, playing along with the game and keeping my voice low, all the while secretly loving having these universally handsome older guys pay attention to me.

Suddenly a version of manhood that I could embody—possibly even successfully—was right in front of me. With my mind now open to the idea of a fraternity, I visited more parties and briefly considered the merits of a few other houses. Sigma Nu guys were pleasant and gentlemanly, but too straight-laced and buttoned-up—starched, tucked-in oxfords instead of the rumpled, untucked look that signaled Phi Psi's moneyed nonchalance. Fiji had the best-looking guys on campus, but rumors were that a lot of them were gay, so that was a nonstarter. And other fraternities had rowdy *Animal House* reputations I wanted no part of. No, it had to be Phi Psi—the slightly athletic but not too burly body type, the casual air of wealth, and the house dog, Norton, with whom I would form a special bond. Finally, I could see my life as a young college man in one coherent frame. I would be one of the smiling guys I'd seen in front of the Phi Psi house, playing Frisbee with Norton in a slightly worn, Greek-lettered T-shirt. I'd pick up a handsome, privileged, even slightly athletic persona all in one neat package, just by signing up.

So I kept attending the parties at Phi Psi, trying to make a connection with any one of the guys I'd met earlier in the week. After rehearsals at night, I'd stop back at the dorm and change into the one alligator shirt I owned, an orange sherbet-colored number I'd picked up on a clearance table at Macy's Action Down Under, before going to the Phi Psi party. By the end of the week, I was a master of small talk. I made jokes about how drunk people got at all the frat parties, talked about Norton the dog as if he and I were already best buds.

Yet just as my conversation and attitude changed as the week wore on, so did the tone of the parties. Whereas it was smiles and handshakes for all on Monday, by Thursday it was serious business. I saw it happening all around me: older guys, members, zooming in on guys my age, but now only ones who had the Phi Psi package—the right clothes, the athletic build, the air of insouciant entitlement. I increasingly found myself on the periphery, the politely tolerated guest, while I watched prospective pledge after prospective pledge be led upstairs for the big conversation. After a night or two of this toward the end of rush week, I took my cue and went back to my dorm, wondering on the short walk across the parking lot and up the stairs what was wrong with me. Why hadn't one of the Phi Psi's put his arm around my shoulder and sought to make me his pledge son, a gesture I would have loved on so many levels?

On the Monday and Tuesday following rush week, as the fourth-floor guys talked about the bids they were receiving from fraternities all over campus, I waited for my letter from Phi Psi. Despite what I had sensed toward the end of the previous week, the writing I'd already seen on the wall, I allowed myself to hope until hope turned to wish, wish turned to longshot, longshot turned to snowball's chance in hell, and snowball's chance in hell turned to cold, hard fact.

"Major fuckheads! You're better off without 'em," Howard said after I told him about the Phi Psi fiasco, which I needed to do because I had told him I was rushing there at Colette's suggestion. Howard thought it was great at first, a real social coup. Then when I told him of my rejection, his attitude about the place turned 180 degrees. He grew caustic and bitter, and I wondered if it brought back his own memories of being burned by fraternity rush.

A month or two into my freshman year, Howard moved out of Sargent and into an off-campus apartment. At Northwestern, it wasn't cool to stay in a dorm beyond sophomore year. If you weren't in a fraternity or sorority, you got an apartment, and only those who didn't have enough money or friends to do that stayed behind. So I understood why Howard left, but I pretty much never saw him after that. I thought about trying to reach him to see if he wanted to get together for coffee or something, but I figured he was probably having fun in his new apartment with his upperclassman friends. Would he really want a freshman who still lived in the dorm hanging around?

Of course, I never found out exactly why I didn't get a bid from Phi Psi. I was not privy to the conversation the brothers had about me in their secret rathskeller, where it was decided I wouldn't fit in. I was left only to imagine it, which I did in all shades of colorful negativity. For the rest of the year, as I'd walk through the fraternity quad in the late afternoon, I'd see a group of guys with the right stuff breezily playing in their Phi Psi T-shirts—smiling, laughing, tossing a football or Frisbee, with Norton the dog running at their feet. I'd stare at some of them a little longer than at others, the way their arms and chests filled out their T-shirts, and my envy would turn to other feelings I still didn't quite recognize for what they were. Gradually, as I found myself bombarded daily by these images of privileged male perfection, I figured it out. I knew exactly why Phi Psi had rejected me and who was to blame.

12

Suffering Artist

Within a month of my arrival at Northwestern, during the week that *Big Time* was set to open, Donna called with the news of two deaths back in New Jersey. My Uncle Ray, who had worked at the Johns-Manville plant during his young adulthood, had died of asbestosis, a lung disease related to the inhalation of asbestos fibers. I'd watched Uncle Ray fade for nearly two years before that, and it rattled me to the bone whenever I saw him, his once commanding six-foot frame reduced before the age of sixty to that of a gaunt, gray specter who lived in his pajamas and struggled to breathe.

The other death was that of Muffet, the eleven-year-old collie-shepherd mix that Benny, Thomas, and I had grown up with since I was seven. Muffet was part of a tortured family history with dogs that stretched back to before I was born, and for most of her life she'd managed to escape the worst of it. The usual life of a Sadowski dog began with my father bringing home a puppy in a cardboard box that "some guy at work" was trying to give away. (I often wondered, was this always the same guy at work?) Yosh usually timed these reveals for when my mother was out of the house, or at least out of the room, but eventually she would find out and hit the roof.

"Goddammit! Who's gonna take care of that thing? It's gonna chew my furniture, shit all over the rug. Get it outta here!"

But even Sophie knew that by the time she'd spoken her peace it was too late. We had already fallen in love with the puppy, held it, named it, brought it dog biscuits and a leash from Aunt Helen's house next door. While Sophie sighed and groaned at the inevitable scenario unfolding in front of her, Yosh grinned and cooed just like one of us kids. Then, inevitably and through no fault of their own, these adorable puppies grew into less cute adult dogs that ended up being bigger than the guy at work had predicted.

Once a dog was full-grown, or even half-grown, Yosh lost interest in it. He insisted that the only place for a dog was outside, chained to a plywood doghouse he would hastily nail together and place in our driveway after my mother had set the conditions under which the dog could stay. Following the cute puppy stage, the Sadowski family dogs that survived lived out their remaining days this way.

But there were also the stories of dogs that Yosh had taken on a "one-way ride," an experience I pictured like that of his pigeons: let go along a highway in Pennsylvania but without the birds' instinct to find their way home. I remember a few puppies from my earlier childhood that I don't remember as adult dogs, animals my father told us he had given away to friends who had "big yards," though I'd never met any of these alleged friends, nor had I ever seen any of their big yards. Once I was old enough, my siblings told me about the one-way rides, and I had to admit to myself that this fate—though I could never confirm it—seemed more plausible than our former dogs having suddenly lucked out into a place in the country with multiple acres to roam.

Yosh threatened Muffet with a one-way ride numerous times, mostly when we played with her in the house, which he had forbidden us to do. But since George had purchased Muffet from a pet store—she hadn't come from the guy at work—and Benny was her primary caretaker, Yosh never dared do it. When Benny went off to Brown, I took over caring for Muffet in my way—feeding her, making sure she always had water, sitting by her doghouse and stroking her head when I got home from school.

Then when I left for Northwestern, I worried about Muffet. She had the gray muzzle hair and limp of an old dog by then. Yosh assured me she would be OK, and my sisters all said they would check on her from time to time. But with her dying so soon after my departure, I couldn't help wondering: had she really had a sudden stroke and died instantly, as Donna told me she did? Or had she been taken on a one-way ride? Or had she just died of loneliness?

Shortly after Donna's phone call—perhaps that night, perhaps a few days later—I had a dream about Muffet, one that recurs to this day. She is lying down on the cement of the driveway, chained to her doghouse as usual. She's emaciated and glassy-eyed, and her water bowl is empty, bone dry. Barely able to pick up her head, she looks at me and lets out a moan that is somewhere between canine and human, pleading for something I desperately, hopelessly want to give but can't understand. Then I wake up.

I didn't cry for Muffet or for Uncle Ray. *Big Time* was opening that weekend, and I had a new life now, one where if I let my eye off the ball for a minute, I could lose a competitive edge and it could all slip away. And what could I have done for either one of them anyway?

I'd come to Northwestern with the goal of eventually becoming a serious film actor or—if that didn't work out—a lead on a soap opera. But after having scored the duet with Colette in *Big Time*, I started thinking musical theatre might be my ticket to stardom, so I auditioned for another student-directed revue. This one was called *Hot Rhythm*, and it featured the songs of Cole Porter.

One of the things I used to hear the *Big Time* cast talk about all the time during rehearsals was how important it was to project energy onstage.

"I *love* Liza Minnelli."

"*Yes!*" someone would reply, jazz hands extended. "She has such great *energy!*"

So when I rehearsed my audition song for *Hot Rhythm*, Porter's "You're the Top," I filled it with energy—*lots* of it. Only afterward did I realize that my wide-eyed facial expressions and arm-swinging, finger-snapping movements probably made me look more like a coke fiend than a musical theatre pro. I didn't get a callback.

In the spring, there were auditions for the *Waa-Mu Show*, the legendary highlight of Northwestern's musical theatre season. Whereas most shows run by the theatre department drew only other theatre students and faculty members as an audience, everyone on campus came to see *Waa-Mu*, an original musical comedy the name of which is based on arcane references to Northwestern history I can never remember. Even the fourth-floor guys had heard of it and asked if I was planning to audition, which of course I was. Underclassmen didn't usually get major roles in *Waa-Mu*—they mostly filled out the ensemble—but if you were a big talent, like Colette, you could land a duet or even a solo. And since I had already sung with Colette, that's what I was gunning for.

There again, no callback—not even for the ensemble—despite the fact that I'd been taking dance classes all year and had dialed back my manic, *Hot Rhythm* audition style quite a few notches. By the end of my first year, I was back in the pack of freshmen who didn't get cast in much of anything (though quite a few freshmen had in fact been chosen for *Waa-Mu*). *Big Time* had proven to be a fluke, and my inferior dance skills seemed an obstacle I could never overcome. So I shifted my attention away from musicals and back toward drama, which allowed me to pooh-pooh *Waa-Mu* and affect the superior air of a serious theatre artist, complete with a pair of darkly tinted John Lennon glasses I wore to create a brooding, distant persona.

At Northwestern, freshmen weren't allowed to take acting classes. Instead, we were required to take a yearlong theatre survey course and work on three stage crews over the course of the year so that we could learn about multiple aspects of the craft (and serve as the free labor that kept the program's productions running). But at the end of your first year in the department, you could interview to get into the acting class of your choice, with which you would usually stay for the next three years. The choice of a teacher was thus a defining moment for every student in Northwestern's acting program, the declaration of a theatrical identity. Having sat in on the different sections, I loved the New York studio feel of a class taught by a revered veteran acting teacher named Victor. In Victor's class, students were doing intense scenes from the great American classics by Miller, Williams, and Albee by the middle of sophomore year.

"Yeah, all the stars are in Victor's class," Howard had once told me with an eye roll when he still lived at Sargent. "The BTPs *love* Victor."

BTPs were "beautiful theatre people" in Howard-speak—juniors and seniors who played lead roles in the mainstage shows and kissed, sometimes on both cheeks, whenever they saw one another. So I signed up for a meeting with Victor, who—except for the hint of a smile he let slip at isolated moments in our interview—lived up to his no-nonsense reputation. A few days later, my throat clenched when I saw a sheet of paper with twenty names posted on Victor's office door—and there was mine. With a flourish of my pen, I proudly initialed the list to accept a spot in Victor's class, and for the second time in my Northwestern acting career, I was on my way, this time to a different theatrical destination. I would never audition for *Waa-Mu* again. Instead, I would study the great classics—Ibsen, Shakespeare, the ancient Greeks. Victor would help me become a real actor, and by the time I was a senior, or maybe even a junior, I'd be a full-fledged BTP.

~

Besides the choice of an acting class, the other high-stakes event that marked the end of freshman year was housing lottery. No longer an incoming student who had to be lured away from Cornell or Penn, I was now at the mercy of the Northwestern housing gods, who—if you committed the sacrilege of pulling a lousy number and didn't have parents who could advocate for you or buy you into a better situation—would banish you to Courtyard, a makeshift dorm that lay a full mile outside campus. I didn't want to stay at Sargent, especially once the theatre cluster members started grouping off and getting apartments. But I hadn't asked anyone to share a place with me, and they hadn't asked me either. So I entered the housing lottery and, among the three-thousand-plus entrants, scored around number three thousand. This meant that even getting back into Sargent was now a pipe dream, and the only housing I could remotely afford was Courtyard.

Being relegated to Courtyard offered one plus in that the plum work-study position of hall monitor—which involved nothing more than sitting at the front desk of a dorm, doing your homework, and making sure no one who didn't live there came in—was easy to come by. I interviewed with Courtyard's building manager, a fifty-something, taciturn Black woman named Gail, who on first impression intimidated me. Gail had large, magenta-tinted glasses and a deep, gravelly voice that I surmised came from sitting in her office all day smoking cigarettes. She said almost nothing during our interview, but she smiled faintly at the end of our brief conversation, and I got the job.

If living on the fourth floor of Sargent made me feel isolated from the theatre students who lived on the second and third floors, living in Courtyard made me feel as if I lived in another galaxy from the rest of human life. Because Courtyard had no dining hall, and hardly anyone was there during the day because it was too far to walk back and forth between classes, I made virtually no friends there. The only person I ever socialized with on any regular basis was a senior English major named Jill, who struck me as worldly and sophisticated—much older than the mere twenty-one she must have been at the time. Jill wore bohemian-looking handknit sweaters and had long brown hair that she tossed back when she let out her deep, throaty laugh. She also had—I think—a pretty good-sized crush on me, though I felt no impulse to reciprocate. Jill would invite me for tea in the late afternoon, and we'd sit in one of the dorm lounges near her room, sip our Earl Grey, and chat wittily about books, mostly the nineteenth-century novels she loved and that had been a staple of the Somerville High School English curriculum. (Jill was thrilled to have met someone else at Courtyard who had actually read *Wuthering Heights* and *The Return of the Native*.)

Jill had another friend named Curtis, a Filipino biology major who was short but built like a small brick house. Curtis almost always wore a tight T-shirt and skimpy athletic shorts, even in winter, and it was evident from the way he looked in them that he spent a lot of time at the gym. Curtis's thigh, arm, and chest muscles did not go unnoticed by me, but they seemed to leave Jill cold, his obvious interest in her going unrequited. Curtis joined Jill and me for tea once, but he had trouble keeping up with our pretentious discourse about Thomas Hardy and the Brontë sisters and stopped coming. But it wasn't the last time he talked to me.

One day while I was sitting at the front desk as hall monitor, I saw Curtis come into the vestibule and fumble for his keycard to enter the building. Through the glass, I noticed all over again how buff he looked in his T-shirt and gym shorts, while being careful not to stare. Finally, Curtis unearthed the keycard from his backpack and walked into the lobby.

"Hi, Curtis," I said, affecting as casually friendly a tone as I could muster. Besides not wanting to let on that I noticed his bulging biceps and rock-hard thighs, I was sensitive to the fact that he might have felt a little left out at our last Victorian literature roundtable.

Curtis said nothing in response. Then, as he walked past me and toward the student mailboxes that lay behind the front desk, he uttered just one word:

"Faggot."

And so it began. Again.

At first, I was worried that Curtis had somehow sensed the way I noticed his body. But I was already pretty good at checking men out surreptitiously, so I figured it was more likely about all the other ways I was apparently still a "faggot": sipping tea with Jill and gushing about Victorian novels, watching the soaps in the Courtyard lounge on afternoons I didn't have class. No one had called me on things like this in more than a year at Northwestern, and I was starting to think that maybe in college nobody cared anymore. Eventually, I concluded that Curtis's hatred toward me was also a lot about Jill and the fact that while Curtis was hot for her, she was hot for me. But the reasons for Curtis's behavior really didn't matter. The bottom line was that I was back to being the straight boy's faggot, Curtis picking right up where Kevin in middle school and Brian in high school had left off.

Whenever I worked the front desk, I was desperate to know whether Curtis was already in the building so that, if he wasn't, I could brace myself for the inevitable assault when he finally walked through the door. If I saw Jill, I might come up with a reason to ask her whether she had seen him, because the hardest part of it all was the uncertainty. Would Curtis suddenly enter the building and reduce me to faggot dust yet again?

If Curtis was in a hurry as he walked by, he might just throw me a quickie:

"Faggot."

If he had more time, he would take advantage of my captive status at the front desk and try to engage me in a conversation about my faggotness, always sotto voce.

"You're such a faggot! Why don't you just admit it? You're a fuckin' fag. Admit it. Don't you know you're a fag?"

I thought about telling Curtis that I knew the reasons he hated me were all about Jill and his jealousy, but I said nothing. First, I couldn't believe this was happening again. This was *fucking college*, for Christ's sake, and here I was the target of yet another bully, who seemed just as obsessed with making sure I knew I was a faggot as the *children* who had done this to me years before. Second, I'd learned from experience that anything I might say would only be twisted around and used against me. But more than anything, there were all the shameful things I was thinking and feeling—sometimes even about Curtis himself—that I was afraid might somehow come out if we started talking, and I'd end up giving him the very confirmation he was looking for.

Though I didn't realize it, Gail must have left her smoke-filled office at least once or twice and overheard what was going on between Curtis and me at the front desk. One afternoon, right after one of Curtis's fag lashings, she stepped into the lobby and asked me to come back to her office with her to talk. Was I about to be interrogated by my boss about whether I was, in fact, a faggot?

"Why do you let him do that to you?" Gail asked in her low, gravelly tone through the cloud of Salem 100 smoke that ribboned up from her desk.

"I don't know," I answered. "I guess I just don't know what to say."

"Nobody should have to put up with that. Nobody," she said, with a low, slow shake of her head. "It's not right. It's just not right."

"Yeah, I know."

"Do you want me to say something about it?" she asked. Then, lowering her tone even more and with a hint of a threat, she added, "'Cause I will . . ."

"No, that's okay. I'll handle it."

"Okay," she said, more as a warning than anything else. Because Gail knew what I knew: if neither of us said or did anything about Curtis, nothing would change.

But it did change, if only a little, if only by chance. The exodus of upperclassmen from Sargent played out for a second year, and by winter a spot opened up in my old dorm. Soon I was back on the fourth floor, and though most of the guys from the previous year had moved into fraternity houses, I was grateful to be anywhere but Courtyard.

I still needed the money from my job at the front desk, though, and I didn't want to quit on Gail after she'd been so nice to me. So I hauled myself up to Courtyard in the cold two or three days a week instead of seven. Jill passed by the desk a few times, and we talked about my staying late after work one day so that we could revive our Victorian tea-time, but the plan never materialized. Because of Curtis, I didn't want to spend any more time at Courtyard than I needed to, so Jill's and my friendship fizzled. I definitely saw less of Curtis once I didn't live in the dorm anymore, but once or twice a week he would still walk by the desk, seemingly with the sole purpose of imprinting a single word on my psyche:

"Faggot."

~

Victor ran his acting class like a veteran Broadway director. In contrast to some of the other classes, where students spent most of the first year doing acting exercises—playing inanimate objects or doing silent improvisations before they were allowed to go anywhere near a script—Victor threw us into the deep end of the pool by January: heavy, intense scenes from *Hedda Gabler, A Streetcar Named Desire, Who's Afraid of Virginia Woolf?* When it was your turn to get up in class, you didn't dare come in with anything less than a fully memorized, fully rehearsed, production-ready performance, after which Victor would slowly turn his head toward the rest of the class and ask, "Comments?" before offering his own critique.

My first assignment was August Strindberg's *The Dance of Death*, a dark, rarely performed Swedish play written in 1900 about a marriage that's falling apart. I played Kurt, the wife's cousin and would-be lover, who plots to help her end her marriage by goading her tyrannical, ailing husband into a heart attack. Even for an audience filled with aspiring actors, *The Dance of Death* was a hard sell.

"I thought you made some *interesting choices*," someone might offer tentatively after one of our scenes, squinting and squirming with discomfort while not actually citing any specific "interesting choices" they'd noticed. "But I guess I didn't really feel the *sexual tension* between Alice and Kurt. I didn't really believe you wanted to, you know, sleep with each other."

To say I had no concept of this role, this play, this situation, or the sexual desire I was supposed to be feeling for Cousin Alice would be a gross understatement. In order to be a standout in the Northwestern acting program, I knew I was going to have to do something more than plodding scenes from *The Dance of Death*.

"You are the *king!*" Victor bellowed in my ear on another day in class, as I attempted the role of Creon from Sophocles's *Antigone*. "How dare this young girl question your authority!"

It was one of the rare times Victor was on his feet in the middle of a scene, right onstage with the actors, trying to get a lackluster performance jump-started before he called for comments from the rest of the class. Like all the other parts I took on, I played Creon stiffly, unable even to tap into the stance of power and authority I had affected as Captain Keller in high school. (Where was Amy when I needed her?) Having tried everything else, Victor even instructed me to take off my shirt during the scene, thinking I might feel a sense of virility that would inspire me to show Antigone who was boss. I complied, but the only feeling this strategy brought up in me was body shame—and the desire to kill Victor for making me stand half-naked in front of the entire class.

What I was starting to learn about acting was that you couldn't fake it, at least not completely. Even though acting was based on playing someone other than yourself under imaginary circumstances, you still had to tap into real emotions: sorrow, anger, exuberance, desire. All of these were things I had tried for most of my life *not* to show, or even feel. How was I supposed to play a character who raged, or cried, or burst with enthusiasm, or yearned for someone sexually when in real life, over and over, all I had ever done was try to push these feelings down?

～

After I moved back to Sargent, during the winter of my sophomore year, I started living a secret life on the weekends.

The fourth floor bustled with activity on weekday mornings, as bathrobed freshmen carried their towels and Dopp kits to and from the showers, but it was eerily empty and silent on Friday and Saturday nights, the guys all out to who knows where. Maybe they were at their frat houses, maybe out with their girlfriends, maybe hanging with a group down on Rush Street, the strip in Chicago where I'd heard people went to drink after the free beer of fraternity rush stopped flowing. The fourth-floor guys from my freshman year were now almost all gone, and it was a whole new crew. Having moved in midyear from Courtyard, I was even more the outsider now, the ancient sophomore whom all the freshmen smiled at politely but no one really knew. Other than my roommate, Jonathan, whose parents lived in Chicago and who usually took the El home on weekends, I can't recall a single one of their names.

At 7:30 or 8:00 on these weekend nights, I would start to feel the full weight of the dorm's silence and venture into campus. I'd head first to the theatre building and walk the halls that hummed with hugs and kisses during the day. I'd hope to run into a pair from Victor's class rehearsing a scene, or see a techie I knew from one of my crew assignments painting a set piece or prepping some lighting instruments, but I never did. Then I'd go upstairs to the faculty suites—maybe Victor or another professor would be working late in their office, I thought. Sometimes I'd get a perfunctory greeting through a window from a professor I vaguely knew, a barely visible wave under a dimly illuminated desk lamp, but mostly I wouldn't see anyone at all.

I'd exit the theatre building by the back door and walk up the ramp to Norris, the student center. I'd scan the heads all facing the big-screen TV—seemingly the only other souls with nowhere else to go on a Friday or Saturday night—looking for any familiar face. Then I'd circle the lounge upstairs. Like the fourth floor and the theatre building, Norris would seem utterly and inexplicably deserted. I might see the random stranger, security guard, or front desk attendant, but everyone I knew, everyone who knew me, seemed to have vanished. *Where were they?*

If it was Friday, the library—which was closed on Saturday nights—was next. It would be even more silent than it was during the week, and I could pass at least forty-five minutes wandering the floors of its three towers searching for a chance encounter.

None of this was about looking for sex—I wouldn't have known what to do with a woman *or* a man. But the emptiness of the library on a Friday night made the bathroom stalls a tempting place to relieve myself of the lust I'd felt for the last muscled jock I'd ogled at the gym or the last glistening, shirtless jogger I'd seen on the lakefront whose image, if it had made enough of an impression, I could keep vivid in my memory well into the winter months. Checking and double-checking under the stalls to make sure I was alone, I would complete the deed as silently as possible, flush my shame—the part of it I could—down the toilet, then scan the bathroom one last time on my way out to make sure I'd been unheard.

By around ten o'clock, I would start the walk back to Sargent. Having disappeared for several hours, I could now reappear as if I'd had a night out, and I could kill a little extra time if I took the slower route along the lake. The lakefront, which buzzed with smiling students tossing Frisbees and impromptu outdoor seminars on warm spring days, was a starkly different place on these biting winter nights the Northwestern catalog had never advertised. Even with the hood of my chocolate-brown Sears snorkel coat pulled tight, I could feel the wind whip across my face and hear the cold waves of Lake Michigan churn—a louder, more violent sound than the soft lapping of spring and summer. Sometimes in this harsh but evocative setting, I would try to feel something important, have an epiphany about the meaning of life or the enormity of the universe, experience the kind of grand realization Victor was always trying in vain to get us nineteen-year-olds to understand. I'd wait for the inspiration to boom out a monologue from one of the great tragedies, pretty sure I would be the only one out on the frozen lakefill to hear it. Maybe I'd recite a few lines:

O, that this too, too solid flesh . . .

But once I heard the sound of my own voice, I couldn't bring myself to go on.

On more than one of these winter nights, I would step out onto the barely visible rocks and stare into the black, inscrutable vastness of the lake. Then I'd take a few more steps forward, moving from the rocks along the grassy lakefront to the ones right at the water's edge, where the surge that splashed up often turned to ice, where I knew it would be easy to slip. I would look back at the void of the deserted campus, up at the starless winter sky, south toward the Chicago skyline, its lights signaling something faintly alive that—if it existed at all—seemed a universe away. Then I'd picture myself taking two or three steps more, beyond the outer rocks into the dark, churning water. I knew that if I dropped into the lake I would feel frigid at first, maybe even experience a brief wave of panic when I realized there might be no turning back, but then I wouldn't feel anything.

At the edge of Lake Michigan, I could imagine something that, until this place, this lakefront, I had never been able to envision quite so clearly before—a way out. Out of Northwestern, yes, but also out of so many other things I had been trying to escape for so long—out of feeling like I was alone amid thousands, out of my shameful desires, out of all the voices in my head and the echo they had gathered up into inside me, which sometimes shouted back at me in words but usually just hissed a low gray static that said nothing at all.

Sometimes, too, I would hear the seductive siren call of disappearance, of simply not showing up back at Sargent that night, or in acting class on Monday, or at Courtyard on my next hall monitor shift, or in New Jersey for spring break. At the water's edge, inches from the irrevocable, I would stand both terrified and exhilarated by my own power, by my ability to—in an instant—cut the very ties that, looking back on it, I probably wanted more than anything. How long would it take, I'd wonder, for everyone to realize I was gone? And when they finally figured it out, what would they say?

After a few minutes on this frigid promontory, my mind already halfway underwater, I would hear yet another voice. Where it came from, how it had built up inside me along with all the others, I don't know. Now I can only describe it as adolescent, self-deluded, even ridiculous. But the voice said something like this: maybe everything that was happening to me, and everything that had ever happened before, was the suffering I needed to do for my art. Wasn't emotional pain a prerequisite for greatness? Wasn't it the only way to become a real artist? Hadn't I heard that somewhere—from Victor, or from a movie, or from some conversation in the hallway of the theatre building?

The source didn't matter. As absurd as this voice may have been, it was a voice of hope—faint, conditional, meager hope. It would call me from the edge of the abyss back onto solid ground. It would coax me from the outermost rocks back onto the artificially engineered turf and asphalt jogging trail of the Northwestern lakefill. It would tell me to put one foot in front of the other for one more night and start the walk back to Sargent. Still fighting it a little—still hearing the other voices that wanted to pull me back to the rocks—I would let it guide me home.

~

In the spring, as the ice on the rocks melted and the sun started to shine a little brighter, another escape route came to me in a sudden flash of clarity. Just as I had in high school, I started sending away for college catalogs, and I began plotting a transfer. It was such an obvious solution that I couldn't understand why I hadn't thought of it before. Maybe it was because there was always that new development that sparked a ray of hope—*Big Time*, making it into Victor's class, getting back into Sargent Hall—then disappointed by not fixing everything, by not fixing me.

I sat at the front desk of Courtyard and rifled through my stack of catalogs, read and reread form letters from colleges that sounded like they would be thrilled to have me. Curtis could come into the building and say whatever he wanted to, because it didn't matter anymore. I was leaving.

The deadlines were fast approaching, but even if I had to wait a semester or even a year, I didn't care. Maybe I'd gun for the real Ivy League this time, shun the "Ivy of the Midwest," as Northwestern liked to call itself. Or I'd go further west, to a small liberal arts college like Reed or Occidental, where somebody might actually notice I was there.

That same spring, Victor announced auditions for the first show he would direct on campus in years, a musical revue of Noël Coward scenes and songs called *Oh, Coward!* Acting teacher to the stars that he was, Victor directing any show was a big deal, but this would also be the first show of the fall season and the first to be performed in a new proscenium theatre never before used for a student performance. Even though I was planning to transfer, I did what everyone in all of Victor's classes did: I auditioned. Pretty much all of Victor's students got a callback—he was nothing if not loyal to his own—but when Victor posted the final cast list he had typed up on the Selectric in his office, there were deep cuts. True to the rumors that had circulated, he took only six performers for the show. And, from our sophomore acting class of twenty, Victor cast only two people: a girl named Julia—who everyone thought was hilarious and who would later go on to star on numerous sitcoms and win more Emmy awards than she could fit on a mantelpiece—and me.

Victor held the first cast meeting in the spring, before everyone left for summer break, and I had no idea what I was going to do. Dozens, probably more than a hundred students all over campus would have given anything to be in Victor's show, and I was just going to walk away because I was transferring? At the meeting, Victor gave us the breakdown of scenes and musical numbers and shared the production concept for the show, which included an art deco set with grand staircases on either side. The men would wear tuxes designed exclusively for them, the women elegant gowns. Julia and I would sing a comic duet called "Why Do the Wrong People Travel?" playing an upper-crust British couple who look down their noses at tacky American tourists. And I would get a solo (my first ever), a romantic ballad called "You Were There," which I would croon while slowly walking down one of the staircases of the glittering art deco set.

That night, I walked back to Sargent pondering this completely unanticipated wrench in my plans. Then, back at the dorm, feeling a mix of triumph and trepidation, I threw all the transfer applications and catalogs in the trash.

13

Straight Man

Oh, Coward! played to packed houses. As the first show ever in the newly christened Josephine Louis Theater, it drew crowds at every performance. With just three weeks between the day we returned the fall of my junior year and opening night, the rehearsal period was brisk. It also was much less grueling than I had come to expect from Victor based on his boot-camp-like approach to actor training, which began with an hour of muscle-splitting calisthenics every morning at 8 a.m.

Classmates were generous in their praise of "You Were There," which I sang decked out in a custom-built tux and which was staged, as promised, on a grand staircase built by Northwestern's professional-grade set crew. Julia and I drew some laughs during "Why Do the Wrong People Travel?" and were, for a day or two after the show, the two biggest BTPs in our acting class.

In the winter, I was cast in *Say Goodnight, Gracie,* a five-character comedy in which I played Jerry, an unemployed actor who refuses to go with his friends to their ten-year high school reunion because he feels like a failure. Doing *Gracie,* I discovered a comic type I could actually be decent at playing—the straight man who takes himself too seriously while all the zanies around him drive him crazy.

I was able to replace my Courtyard hall monitor job, and thus get rid of Curtis completely, with a paid internship at Northlight, the main professional theatre in Evanston, walkable from campus. Working under the artistic directors and any guest artists brought in to direct shows, I scheduled auditions, read opposite actors who needed to run lines, and prepared scripts for rehearsals. I got to work with a lot of big Chicago theatre names, including John Malkovich, who directed two shows during my internship. It was a job just about all of my Northwestern theatre peers would have killed to have, one time that being eligible for federal work-study worked to my advantage.

Just when I feared I would have to set up house with a stranger in my junior year, I got an off-campus apartment with Chris, a resident of the original Sargent fourth floor, who I serendipitously heard was looking for a roommate.

Then in my senior year, I got the male lead in Lanford Wilson's *Balm in Gilead*, a contemporary drama that a lot of people auditioned for because it was directed by Ann, a popular young acting teacher, and because everyone knew it would have a cool, edgy vibe. The central character was Joe, a guy who gets in over his head dealing drugs in the late-night underworld of New York City. Ann set the show to a soundtrack of Bruce Springsteen's *Born to Run* and issued an advisory at the callbacks that Joe was going to have a nude scene. At one point in the play, at least in our production, Joe bolts out of the bed he shares with his girlfriend when he realizes he's missed a meeting with a dealer to whom he owes a lot of money. After getting dressed, Joe rushes back down to the streets while the ominous strains of Springsteen's "Jungleland" play in the background.

The fact that *Balm in Gilead* would include a nude scene created a buzz in the department—this was, after all, the buttoned-up 1980s—and having survived my turn as a half-naked Creon in Victor's class, I figured I might as well go all the way. Ann staged the scene tastefully on a platform at the rear of the Wallis Theater, the black box where the show was performed. When I got up from the bed, it was obvious that I wasn't wearing anything, but distance and dim lighting gave the scene more the feel of stark, modern realism than pornography (or at least that's what I told myself). Peers congratulated me for my let-it-all-hang-out courage, the show lived up to its preproduction hype, and *Balm in Gilead* became a hip new credit I could add to the respectable acting résumé I was starting to build up.

For the first time since arriving on campus, I also made a few close friends. One of these was Patti, one of the few people ever to ask me to be their scene partner in acting class, instead of it always being the other way around. Halfway through my junior year, I switched acting teachers from Victor to another popular teacher named David, ostensibly because I was looking for a more process-oriented approach. (Though I was also angry at Victor for not casting me in his second play. Apparently, the solo he'd given me in *Oh, Coward!* wasn't enough.) Patti was one of the best actors in David's class. She had great comic timing that I could pick up the rhythm of whenever we worked together, and when the class studied British black comedy, we knocked 'em dead with scenes from Joe Orton and Harold Pinter.

The other friend I made was Gerri, a barely five-foot-tall Brooklynite who was a year ahead of me in the theatre program and whose circle of friends consisted primarily of gay men. While not-so-secretly crushing on several of them (including, as I would eventually learn, me), Gerri played up the role of Jewish mother to her following, who could be found at her apartment at virtually any hour of the day or night playing cards, smoking cigarettes, or downing shots of Jack Daniels. With or without an invitation, I was always welcome at the never-ending party that was Gerri's apartment, where I positioned myself as the nonsmoking, moderately drinking "straight one." All the guys had women's names they used for one another when they were catting it up—Margie, Beulah, Gerri's roommate Frank was Francesca. I joined in the banter a lot of the time and ended up with my own drag name, Stella, but it never stuck. (Was it because I was ostensibly "the straight one" and everyone, being sensitive to my still-closeted sensibilities, was careful not to push it?) When the gang was going to the Bistro, a gay dance club in Chicago, I found a million reasons to beg off. I'd say I had "something I had to do" or, because it was usually midnight by the time the big gay caravan started rolling down Lake Shore Drive, an early class or rehearsal the next morning.

I also started going on dates with women and had one experience that could even be called a romantic relationship. Instead of going back to New Jersey the summer between my junior and senior years, I stayed in Evanston and was cast in a nonunion production of *Tartuffe* at a small theatre in Chicago. Another cast member, Laura, had a car and often gave me rides home late at night. Laura was five years older than me, twenty-five to my twenty, and was already dating a guy named Jack. But Laura and Jack had an open relationship, at least until he got back from doing summer stock in New England. Laura and I kissed in her car for thirty, sometimes forty-five minutes when she dropped me off after rehearsals. We had picnic lunches on the lakefront and long talks about what our careers would be like in five years' time. I would tell her about my dreams of moving to Los Angeles, where a career in movies or television was actually starting to seem possible.

Taken all together, I was living what some might call—what even I might call looking back on it—a charmed life. Things were going my way theatrically, socially, even for a time romantically. Between rehearsals, outings with friends, and picnics with Laura, I didn't have much time to think about stepping back out onto the rocks and dropping into Lake Michigan. But the voices that had brought me there were still inside me. Like someone who loses two hundred pounds yet still sees a heavy person in the mirror, I experienced my halcyon days in college not as an upperclassman enjoying the hard-earned fruits of his first two years' labor but as the isolated misfit I still felt myself to be. Every friendship felt precarious, every role a director's mistake they would later come to regret, every date with a woman a lie, especially to myself. And I was sure that if anyone ever saw who I really was, everything I'd built would come crashing down around me.

~

Even in the 1980s, out gay men were all over Northwestern. Theatre students, non-theatre students, professors, they seemed to be everywhere, especially in Gerri and Frank's apartment on any given night. The constant presence of something you don't want to be but somewhere inside know you are forces you to do one of two things: give in or define yourself in opposition to it. You're either with them or you're against them.

Curtis, Phi Psi, everything that had happened before—it all added up to my answer. Just as I had when I found Benny's love letter on the dresser, I took the gay part of myself and pushed it back into the furthest corner of my consciousness. What had that part of me ever done but expose me to ridicule, disdain, or, at best, polite rejection? And while I was at it, I also pushed the part of myself that was the son of an alcoholic, factory-working, pigeon-racing Legionnaire back into this same corner of my psyche. What had *that* ever done for me but get me rejected from fraternities and condemn me to feeling like I would never be good enough to fit in anywhere (or at least anywhere I wanted to fit in)?

But somebody still had to go to class and show up at rehearsals. Somebody had to hang out at Gerri's apartment and play the role of the straight man, even if no one else bought the act. Somebody had to date the young women of Northwestern. Somebody had to put on a tuxedo and sing a romantic ballad on a grand staircase, even if he had no idea who or what he was singing about. So I invented another self, and he finished college for me. He had a pretty good run, but there were cracks in his armor, especially when it came to women.

The dates he went on all felt prematurely aborted, certainly to him and no doubt even more so to the women he courted. He made a valiant effort with Natalie, a year behind him in the theatre program. Natalie was pretty and sweet, with wide brown eyes and a buoyant air—the perfect casting choice for the role—and she seemed dazzled by his status as an upperclassman who had performed on the Northwestern mainstage. Everything went fine on their first date. She even seemed happy with the quick kiss he planted on her lips as he dropped her off in front of her dorm. But as their second date approached, a weight started to bear down on him. He knew a quick peck on the lips at the end of the night was only going to cut it for so long. This wasn't the middle school world of "going with" someone, holding hands in the hallway between classes and going on the occasional date to the bowling alley. There were expectations. And the usually sunny, I'm-nice-to-everybody Natalie seemed testy by the end of their third date, when the quick peck on the lips was still all he had to deliver.

What's wrong with me? she probably wondered. *Does he even like me?*

He wanted to do more, or at least he *wanted to want* to do more. So he called Natalie to give it another try. He left a message with her roommate. She left a message back, and then he called again and left another message. Message after message, but now they were a week apart instead of just a few days, until it was obvious there wasn't going to be another date. He felt the weight lift off his chest. For at least a few more weeks, until the next eligible potential girlfriend came along, he wouldn't have to go out on any dates at all. And he wouldn't have to wonder what he was going to do when they were over.

Laura was the exception. What he felt with Laura when they kissed or when they had long talks during their afternoon picnics or late night car chats was real. The adrenaline rush, the tingle in his limbs, it was there, *it was working.* He was a real boyfriend, finally fulfilling his purpose, almost a man. Why did it work with Laura when it didn't with the others? Maybe it was the fact that she was older and therefore safer—they both knew it would probably never last. Or maybe it was the prospect of Jack coming back at the end of the summer, a finite end that made the fling a lark instead of a test, which—he admitted to himself in his most private moments—was the way it felt with the others.

Once and only once, Laura invited him to spend the night at her apartment in downtown Chicago. They went to bed as planned, she serving as patient and willing guide to the young novice. He performed more or less successfully but mechanically, like a figure skater who gets the technical elements right but whose artistry is lacking. A week later, Jack was back in town—and he felt the familiar weight lift off of him again.

~

I remember surprisingly little from my trips back to New Jersey during my four years of college. I have a vague memory of the first Thanksgiving reunion of my high school friends, that time everyone comes back in their respective insignia and says how great everything is at Northwestern or Duke or Delaware or Georgetown. I don't remember any subsequent reunions, though I'm sure we had them.

I remember the job my sister Donna arranged for me at the bank where she worked the first two summers I came home.

I remember visiting the starter home Nancy and Mark bought in Manville after having rented for a few years. It was the end of the summer before I was to set up my first off-campus apartment. Nancy and Mark had a lot of household supplies they wouldn't be using in their new place, and she loaded me up on pots and pans, unbreakable dishes, a toaster, towels, and other things she obviously had spent hours gathering and cleaning.

"I don't know if you'll want this," she said, as she showed me each item she had laid out on her kitchen counter.

I remember the lump in my throat, the almost-but-not-quite crying, as I drove away with the stash in the trunk of Yosh's car. And the next day, I remember stuffing it all into my super-sized duffel bag and flying back to Chicago, where rehearsals for *Oh, Coward!* were about to begin.

I remember the day Kathy handed me a bundle of bills she and Joe had saved up, $110, at the end of my senior year. She said they thought

I might need it to "get started" after college. I did, of course, and I remember how, when the bills transferred from my hand to my wallet, I felt the now-familiar lump form in my throat again.

But I don't remember anything else from those holiday breaks or summer vacations. I don't hold a single memory of a conversation with my father during my four years of college, though we must have talked to each other. He still owned the house on Lincoln Avenue, and I stayed there every time I was back in town. But it's as if my mind separates these two worlds now just as I kept them separate then—Lincoln Avenue was the past, the life I had merely been forced to live for seventeen years. Northwestern was what mattered, the place where I was creating the new, real me.

~

As June of senior year approached, my classmates started buzzing with news of their families coming out to Evanston for commencement. All the worldly, sophisticated BTPs were suddenly children again, eager to have Mom and Dad meet their professors and cheer in the stands as they received their diplomas. Seamus and Lane, two guys who had been roommates in the Sargent theatre cluster and who now shared an apartment off campus, invited me to an afternoon cocktail party they were having with graduates and their visiting parents. Suddenly, something occurred to me that hadn't ever before: Was I supposed to invite Yosh to graduation?

No one from my family had ever come out to see any of my shows at Northwestern. I hadn't minded this, because it had never even occurred to me that they would. It was eight hundred miles from New Jersey. But the fact that *everybody's* parents seemed to be coming out for commencement had me in a panic. Lane had invited me and "my parents" to his and Seamus's party as if it were the most natural thing in the world—of course I had parents coming to graduation, and of course we would love to stop by the party. But the images this simple invitation conjured were nothing Lane could have imagined.

At the cocktail party in my mind, I pictured Yosh in his paint-splotched work clothes trying to hobnob with the WASPy parents of my classmates. I'd be watching his every move, listening to his every word for the faux pas that would force me to intervene and then make a hasty, apologetic exit. It would be Archie Bunker sharing cocktails and conversation with Ward and June Cleaver, or the Lawrences from *Family*. He would have too many highballs, attempt to regale everyone with stories about his glory days as a pigeon racer, tell a group of bluebloods from Greenwich or Grosse Point what a "fart smeller" I was to be graduating from Northwestern. (Would he even get the name of the university right?) This was, of course, something I could never let happen. Never in any of my visits or phone calls home had I mentioned the possibility of my father's flying out to Chicago, and I wasn't about to do it now that graduation was coming. To my great relief, he never mentioned it either.

At the all-campus ceremony on graduation day, I served as my own audience and cheering section. I took in the significance of the moment as both participant and spectator, as if I were marching in my cap and gown while also watching myself from the stands of Northwestern's Dyche Stadium. I thought about my four years of college, about everything that had brought me to the rocks, about everything that had happened both before that and after. And I smiled. It didn't matter that I was alone while my classmates all left the stadium under the arms of their parents, bouquets of flowers in their hands. I knew that in just a few days, I would be in a car headed to California.

I wasn't going to LA to launch my movie career just yet—that was going to have to wait. A few weeks before graduation, I had been cast at a new summer stock theatre on California's Russian River, about ninety miles north of San Francisco. The season would consist of three musicals, starting with Stephen Sondheim's *A Little Night Music*. In less than a week, the entire cast, plus a director, musical director, and stage manager—all hired from Chicago—would form a caravan of cars and drive halfway across the country.

On the afternoon of graduation day, the School of Speech, of which theatre was one of about a half-dozen departments, conferred its degrees at Pick-Staiger Concert Hall, directly behind the theatre building that my classmates and I had all made our second home. I was relieved that there was a separate section for parents so that I, the cheese, didn't have to stand alone again. We sat by department and within that, in alphabetical order so that we could all go up onto the stage and receive our diplomas in an orderly fashion. "DavidSarantinotheatreNewJersey," whom I'd met my very first day on campus, was at my side.

The degree recipients in theatre were called to the stage one by one. I knew all of them, and we cheered for each other, the forty-plus die-hards who had entered the program four years earlier and stuck it out. When my name was called, people who had been in the Sargent theatre cluster, Victor's class, David's class, *Oh, Coward!*, *Say Goodnight, Gracie*, and *Balm in Gilead* applauded and cheered for me. A few shouted my name.

During the ten seconds that were my moment on the Pick-Staiger stage, I looked out into the auditorium and saw forty smiling faces, open with what looked like genuine affection. And in that moment, I wondered if maybe I had been at least a little bit wrong. Maybe I had been part of something after all.

After the ceremony, while the families all gathered for dinners and celebrations, I went back to my apartment and packed for California.

～

The following Monday, the white Chrysler that was to be my ride out west showed up in front of my Evanston apartment, the other cars in the caravan directly behind it. As we pulled away, I looked back, but only at the other vehicles. In a few short days, we would all be on the Russian River, which I would soon learn ranks with Provincetown, Fire Island, and Key West as one of the top resort destinations in the United States for gay men. At most of the resorts on the Russian River, nude sun-bathing around the pool was common, and any man you passed on the street, who waited on you in a restaurant, or who stood behind you in line at the Safeway could just be assumed to be gay.

Just a few days after graduation, this was where the straight man was headed.

PART THREE

VOICES

To have a voice is to be human. To have something to say is to be a person. But speaking depends on listening and being heard. It is an intensely relational act.

—CAROL GILLIGAN

A body is a body, but only voices are capable of love.

—RICARDO PIGLIA

14

Lover

My first sexual encounter with a man began with a cheesy line out of a gay porn film.

The evening had started with a sparsely attended performance of *A Little Night Music*, which ran for the entire summer when the producers ran out of money to mount the rest of the season. As part of an effort to placate the cast and crew for a change of plans that left us all feeling a little baited and switched, the production company gave us free access to the bar in the back of the theatre after hours. Get them drunk and they won't complain, I guess was the thinking.

The Russian River, with its open gay sexuality everywhere, had gradually loosened up our band of young actors and techies, freshly carted in from the Midwest. And on this fateful night, the usual glass of wine after a performance evolved into a company-wide drinking binge, which was then followed by some nude kissing and groping in the living room of the men's residence. As it has always tended to be throughout my life, my response to a significant amount of alcohol was to fall asleep, and I missed all the fun, in which I might actually have taken part had I been able to stay awake. (The free spirit of the river had worked its way into my consciousness, too.) But my castmate Will, with whom I shared a bedroom, *had* managed to stay awake. When he came in for bed at the end of the night, I woke up and immediately remembered what had transpired earlier in the evening.

"So how was it?" I asked provocatively from under my bed sheets.

"*Interesting . . .*" Will answered coyly. "And then Jamie threw up."

"Oh my God!" I said, now fully awake.

"He was barfing into the bowl for a long time," Will went on. "But he's all right now. It's all cleaned up. I took care of him."

Then, with a fearlessness I don't understand to this day and the most suggestive, porn-movie delivery I could muster (even though I'd never seen a porn film), I came back with my come-on line:

"So . . . do you want to take care of *me* now?"

And my first sexual encounter with a man ensued.

~

Will was tall, blond, and handsome, but not necessarily someone I would have been particularly drawn to under normal, non-summer-stock circumstances. His physique was thinner than the football player/wrestler body type that usually got my attention, and he had a trenchant wit played in a distinctly gay key, which—because I was still 99 percent in the closet—made me squirm a little. But Will made me feel things I didn't know it was possible to feel. We started sleeping together that very night, as every trepidation I'd ever had about gay sex instantly fell away. It didn't feel shameful or confusing or even profound, all the things I might have expected it to feel after twenty-one years of denial. It just felt obvious and really, *really* good. So *this* is what all the fuss over sex is about, I thought. *Of course I'm gay*, said something inside me when a level of pleasure I'd never known coursed through my body.

Because Will and I shared a room, we were able to carry on a secret affair for the rest of the summer simply by closing our bedroom door every night. And though I had fleeting moments when I wondered just what it all meant, the new sensations I was feeling told me not to look back.

Then in late August, the summer of sunshine, Sondheim, and sex was over, and I faced a dilemma. I was becoming obsessed with Will and our nightly trysts, which I seemed to need more, not less, as the summer wore on. But Will's plan was to go to New York, wait tables at his old restaurant job in the West Village, and live with his parents on Long Island while he figured out his long-term future. I, on the other hand, had planned to stay in California, and after being there for a couple of months my desire to live there was based on more than just romantic fantasy and the wish to be as far away from Lincoln Avenue as possible. I loved the crystal blue skies, the scrubby red mountains of Marin and Sonoma counties, the seemingly endless sunshine, the crisp, cool air and waterfront vistas of San Francisco. The plan was I'd start in the Bay Area doing theatre and commercial work and sign up with an agent that my former classmate Robin, who grew up in Berkeley, had worked with in her teens. Once I accumulated some professional credits in San Francisco, I'd then move south to LA, where I'd become a TV and movie star by the age of twenty-five.

In the end, money—not romance or even sex—proved to be the determining factor in my decision. Our stock salaries barely got us through the summer, and I had no money for a security deposit on an apartment in San Francisco, nor did I have any job prospects. To make the choice even clearer, Jerome, our director, was giving his car as a hand-me-down to his sister, Shelley, who lived in New York. He needed someone to drive the car cross-country, so he asked if Will and I might want to use it as our mode of transportation back east. As much as I really, *really* didn't want to go back to Lincoln Avenue, at least I could live there rent-free until I made enough money to get my own place in the city. So after a brief detour to drop Jerome off at his father's house in Hollywood, which struck me as dirtier and much less glamorous than I'd expected, Will and I took our secret affair on the road, into the Travelodges, Motel 6s, and Super 8s that dotted the I-20 corridor.

Five days and two roadside breakdowns after our departure from LA, Will and I pulled up in front of the Upper West Side restaurant where Shelley had suggested we meet. We shared a quick drink with her and handed her the keys. Then we stepped out onto Columbus Avenue and looked at one another nervously in the late afternoon sun, having talked not at all about what was going to happen next.

"So where are you headed now?" I asked Will, hoping the New York chapter of our romance would begin at precisely that moment with a candlelit dinner and a lovemaking session in some still-undetermined hotel room in the city.

"Well—I have to stop by work and let them know I'm back in town," Will said. "I need to get my schedule, you know. And then I have to go see my parents."

"Okay, maybe I'll call you tonight then."

"Hmmm. I'm not sure when I'll be home, so maybe tomorrow? Or toward the weekend?" Then, in a chummy tone that sounded more like that of a buddy than a lover, he said, "Yeah—we'll get together."

And we did, a few times for dinner or coffee or a drink. I don't remember. I do remember that we visited each other once at our respective houses, ending up in his parents' bed one night and on my father's couch another, the danger of both situations temporarily rekindling a flame that had otherwise pretty much burned out. Mostly, I remember the phone calls during which I felt the ache of not having something that had finally made me feel OK, and then the ache of those phone calls becoming less and less frequent. Though Will would never say it, it was becoming apparent that to him, we had been a fun summer fling, sprung out of the insular world unto itself that was stock theatre, and now he was ready to get on with real life. For me, our time together had changed me at the core, allowed me to experience something that felt like happiness. Without him, all I would be left with was myself again— and now, for the first time in four years, my father.

～

"Why do you have to go to damn New York every day?"

Yosh bombarded me with this question one morning while concealing his breakfast highball under the kitchen table, as if I hadn't figured out that trick years earlier. He started this conversation just as I was headed out the back kitchen door, trying to catch the 7:25 bus into the city.

"There's jobs around here," he added to bolster his case.

After four years in college, despite the fact that I probably hadn't gotten much taller, the house and its rooms felt smaller now, the ceilings lower, the walls closer in than I'd remembered them. Yosh had quit pigeon racing years earlier, but the coop was still in the backyard. The time Will came out to visit me, I made sure he did so under cover of night and that he parked his car on the street so that his headlights wouldn't reveal any of its mustard-colored ugliness.

Yosh was sixty-five now, and he seemed smaller, too, less formidable, his criticisms of my life choices easier to dismiss. And maybe I was stronger, twenty-one now, emboldened by the knowledge that with my Northwestern bachelor's degree in hand, I could move out the minute I earned enough money to put down a month's rent and security deposit.

A few other things had changed, too. Yosh had recently retired and was living on Social Security. He didn't offer the tens and twenties from his wallet as readily as he had when I was in high school, and I took them even less frequently, determined to prove that I didn't need his money and could make it on my own. He drank more at home than at the bars he'd frequented in his younger years, and without a job to go to, he was now downing hard liquor all day. He had started talking with my sisters about moving in with Elaine and selling the house, but they convinced him to keep it at least until I graduated. (Somehow they knew, despite my protestations to the contrary, that I might come crawling back after college and need a place to stay.)

Then, of course, there was the big, gay elephant in the kitchen. Thankfully, Yosh couldn't ask me anymore, as he had virtually every year throughout middle and high school, if I was planning to go out for football. But based on his dogged determination to man me up when I was younger, I concluded that I could never tell him I was gay. The disgust I imagined he would express was something I refused to subject myself to, and I was pretty sure he would never ask because he either didn't have a clue or didn't want to know—I could never be sure which.

"Jobs? Around here? Like where?" I shot back, resentful of his starting this conversation when I was already running late.

"I don't know. At the bank or somethin'," Yosh answered, undaunted by my impatient tone. "There's jobs."

"At the *bank*? Do you think that's what I went to college for? To work at a bank?"

"Well you prob'ly spend all the money you make on that goddamn bus. What the hell's the point?"

"I need to be in the city so I can go to auditions."

"Go to *what*?"

"Never mind. I have to go to work."

I closed the door hard and headed into the city, leaving Yosh sitting at the kitchen table, drinking.

~

On a tip from Gerri, who'd moved back to Brooklyn after graduating from Northwestern, I'd registered with a temp agency in Midtown and had gotten a job in the office of, ironically, a bank. It was a grim seven-to-seven commute, and I probably could have gotten a similar job in Jersey, but that would have been to admit defeat—and cave in to Yosh's exhortations—before I'd even started trying to build an acting career. Having a Manhattan work address meant that I could, in theory at least, use my lunch break to visit agents and casting directors and go on auditions.

As it turned out, the one hour I got off in the middle of the day at my temp job left little time for anything but running downstairs for a sandwich and coffee and maybe scanning the ads in *Backstage* for auditions I didn't have the time, energy, or nerve to attend. What I learned pretty quickly is that the New York acting world is an overwhelming sea of mostly closed auditions, 99 percent of which are inaccessible to people who don't have a card from Actors' Equity or one of the TV or film unions. But you can't get a union card without a union job, thus the catch-22 that beginning actors are always complaining about. There are ways to crack the system if you have enough tenacity and belief in your own talent to show up anyway and not let repeated slammed doors and unreturned phone calls wear you down. And of course, this was not me. So instead of the career I'd planned after graduating from Northwestern's nationally renowned acting program, I was one of a busful of cranky commuters heading in and out of the Lincoln Tunnel every day, entertaining dreams of an acting career but with no concrete plan whatsoever for making those dreams a reality.

The exception to this day-to-day drudgery was Friday nights, when I would meet Gerri at O'Neal's Balloon, an after-work bar and restaurant—emphasis on the bar—across Columbus Avenue from Lincoln Center. Gerri had started hanging out at O'Neal's because it was close to where her best friend, Paul, worked. And one night, with the Tanqueray and Jack Daniels flowing and the jukebox blaring Michael Jackson, Pat Benatar, and Huey Lewis, O'Neal's seemed a good place to slip a piece of information to Gerri that she would barely be able to hear. Despite the fact that Will and I were over, I knew I was never going back to being "straight." Gerri seemed the safest person to tell, and this the safest place to do it.

"So—this actor Will and I had kind of a thing while we were in California," I said, after deliberately positioning myself in front of the jukebox's deafening speakers.

"So, are you saying you're gay?" Gerri asked, smirking and looking not at all fazed by a revelation I'd contemplated for weeks.

"I guess so. Or maybe I'm bisexual—I'm not really sure—but—I guess so."

"Uh huh."

"Does that surprise you?" I asked, though her knowing grin had already given me the answer.

"Not really. Well—I've sort of suspected for a while."

"I guess I feel a little silly telling you this after all this time."

"Oh, please—I've heard it all before," she said, holding up her Virginia Slim at a blasé angle. "Different people come out at different times and in different ways. It's certainly OK by me."

Then the rest of the evening went on, just like all the other Friday nights we'd spent at O'Neals. My big first coming out, which I'd been waiting for even as I was dreading it, turned out to be a nonevent. Nothing with Gerri changed at all after that, until things with her friend Paul did. At some point, Gerri had obviously told Paul that I'd come out to her because Paul suddenly started taking more of an interest in me: chatting me up, finding ways to break away from conversations with other people at the bar, flirting. Paul was short, blond, skinny, and twinkishly cute in a way that drives a lot of gay men crazy but, again, was not particularly my type. But I basked in his attention, especially having recently been jilted by Will, and went with it to a point while also keeping a safe distance, because I knew Gerri was desperately in love with Paul.

One night, after the three of us had had too many cocktails and it was too late for me to catch the last bus back to Jersey, we all crashed in Gerri's queen-size bed in Brooklyn. Just as I was drifting off to sleep, I felt Paul's leg brush up against mine, first at the ankle, then a little further up. Then it wasn't just my leg anymore that Paul was touching, and then it wasn't just him doing the touching. Paul and I spent the rest of the night making out—more or less silently, I hoped—while Gerri slept, or at least pretended to.

~

Gerri's reaction to Paul's and my becoming a couple moved through at least five stages of grief. She went from disbelief to hurt to outrage to acceptance (or at least resignation) to an if you can't beat 'em, join 'em attitude, in which the three of us hung out like musketeers until bedtime, when she was once again the odd girl out. I felt horrible about how Paul's and my unexpected romance instantly left Gerri an outsider in a friendship circle of which she had previously been the hub. But with the void Will's absence from my life had opened up inside me, I couldn't resist how Paul looked at me, the compliments he paid me, the things he seemed to see in me that I could never see in myself. He told me I was handsome, he told me I was smart, he wanted me sexually almost every night, with an ardor I had never felt from Will, except maybe on that first night in our twin-bedded room on the Russian River. Had I been programmed differently, Paul's adoration might have led me to see myself through new eyes. But the twenty-two years I'd lived up to that point wouldn't let that happen.

When a young man who has lived in denial for years finally gives in to the fact that he is sexually attracted to men, one might expect the sex act itself to cause all the emotional turmoil—the guilt, the shame, the constant need to cover one's tracks, the feeling that one is doing something—*is* something—dirty. I think that's what I secretly and sadly expected my entire life to be like one day, but it didn't turn out that way at all. When Will and I were together, something within my body changed, miraculously made everything OK, literally overnight. But eventually, the sex and the feeling of being OK that came with it were gone, because Will was gone. I was back to just being the person I'd been before. And that person had to learn to believe another man could love him. Compared to that, accepting my sexuality had been easy.

Paul was an upper-middle-class WASP from a somewhat fancy suburb of Cleveland. His clothing style was Brooks Brothers preppy, which in the eighties simultaneously marked you as blue blooded and on trend. His family had a lake house in New Hampshire that he talked about all the time—the waterskiing, the hilarious antics with the wealthy and WASPy aunts, uncles, and cousins. I'm sure I inflated the poshness of the whole scene in my mind, but whenever Paul regaled me with stories of this world, all I heard were the voices inside me saying I wasn't good enough for it. And I decided that was Paul's real objective. After all, wasn't that what every man I'd ever known wanted in the end, to make me feel bad about myself?

I didn't let Paul meet anyone from my family except Benny, who by then was living with his boyfriend, Tim, in the respectable suburb of Morristown, New Jersey—no pigeon coops for miles. I'd never said to Benny, "I'm gay," and he'd never said it to me, but at some point we must have come to some kind of tacit understanding. (I *certainly* never told him about the letter I found on his dresser and read. Decades later, as I write this, I still haven't.) I told Benny that I wanted to come out and visit some time because there was "someone I wanted him to meet." So one night, Paul and I took the bus from Port Authority to Morristown, where Benny and Tim had invited us for dinner. There we were, four gay men who were, in a sense, family, and we never once uttered the word "gay."

~

Five months after Paul and I became a couple, Gerri and I found an apartment together in Fort Greene, Brooklyn. I had left Lincoln Avenue a few months earlier and moved into a temporary sublet, and now I was excited to be signing my first New York lease. Against all my wishes and warnings, Paul moved in a couple of months later when his roommate in Manhattan decided to leave town and he couldn't afford to keep their place on his own. Besides the fact that I had already decided that Paul's secret, nefarious plan was to make me feel inferior, I'd also realized after the first few months we were together that he had a serious drinking problem. The slurred speech, the sneaking around to hide the booze reminded me too much of my father. And, even though it never turned into rage directed toward me, Paul's drinking gave me another, more legitimate reason to push him away. Eventually, I moved out to another temporary sublet just to escape the whole situation, found another boyfriend I allowed myself to trust only to a point, and told Paul our relationship was over.

Then my sublet was about to run out. I needed to come back to Fort Greene, so I needed Paul to move out once and for all. We weren't a couple anymore, and the whole thing would have just been too awkward. So one night I went out to the apartment and explained this while he, Gerri, and I sat around the kitchen table.

"So, you'll need to find an apartment, Paul," I said. "I'm sorry about this. I know it's hard to find a place in the city, but you have a few weeks. And Gerri and I can help you . . ."

"Well, actually . . ." Gerri interjected. "Paul and I were talking and— we decided we'd like to take over the lease."

Paul said nothing, he and Gerri apparently having decided in advance that she would do the dirty work. It had not even occurred to me that I, rather than Paul, would be the one to move out. But slowly, the reality of what Gerri was saying sunk in.

"So . . . you want *me* to go instead?"

"No, it's not like that," Gerri said.

"Then what is it like?" I asked, looking straight at her, then at Paul, my head now hot with the boiling sensation of betrayal.

"It's just that . . . you left, and Paul and I have lived together for a while. And we *like* living together."

"So—you're leaving me out on the street then?"

"No—just . . . I love you, but . . ." By now, Gerri was crying.

"But what?" I asked.

Gerri sighed. Then, with a gleam in her eye, almost as if she were delivering a manifesto, she said:

"All my life, I've been in the background and I've never had a chance to grab the brass ring. And I finally feel like I can do that now. I want to live with Paul. *I want the brass ring.*"

And there it was. A shiny, valuable object that symbolized everything Paul was and everything I wasn't. The fact that Gerri had been in love with Paul since before I even moved to New York never factored into my interpretation of what was happening, nor did the fact that I was the one who had walked out first. All I heard in Gerri's metallic metaphor was confirmation of my essential lack of worth. Maybe Gerri really did love me, but she loved Paul more.

After a short, spiteful attempt to wrest the lease away from Gerri and Paul, I relented and got yet another sublet, this time in Manhattan. I shared a cramped one-bedroom with two other guys in the West 50s so that I could save money for a move back to Chicago. I'd heard that a lot of actors after graduating from Northwestern stayed there to get their professional feet wet before attempting to swim in the vast oceans of New York and LA. And since I was, in just about every way, drowning in New York, maybe that strategy could work for me.

So fourteen months after I walked out of the Fort Greene apartment for the last time, I got on a plane with all my possessions and—once again—flew west.

15

Actor

Chicago, looking west from Lake Shore Drive, has arguably the most picturesque skyline in the United States. The skyscrapers of Dearborn, Wabash, and Michigan Avenues, set back from the Drive by the parks and plazas that run along Lake Michigan, are spread out in a wide-angle cityscape that accentuates each one's distinctive architecture and makes the denser skylines of New York and San Francisco look crowded, even cluttered by comparison.

From this vantage point, in a car I'd rented at Midway Airport and filled with my modest collection of worldly possessions, a newcomer's thrill stirred in me as I drove north and gazed at the benevolent city that would soon welcome me into its fold. Here, I thought, I could make my mark and be noticed. Here, I would finally have a chance to be an actor, instead of being caught in the catch-22 that was the New York theatre and film scene. Here, I could rent a one-bedroom apartment for less than the cost of my cramped three-way share in Manhattan. Here, I could find the love of my life or, better still, he could find me.

The apartment I chose was in Rogers Park, the farthest-north neighborhood along the lakefront, mostly because rents were low there but also because it was closest to the familiar world of Northwestern that lay just over the city line in Evanston. Though much less meticulously landscaped and maintained than Evanston, Rogers Park still had the brick courtyard buildings, abundant green space, and lakefront access of its fancier neighbor to the north, but at a fraction of the cost. And living on the Chicago side of the line—in addition to signaling that I was now a grown-up city slicker—meant being on the main El train line, which I would need easy access to for auditions, rehearsals, and whatever job I found downtown to pay the bills.

My new place was enormous by New York standards—it even had a dining room—but it was Chicago-style, no-nonsense basic. It was two flights up over a courtyard that consisted only of grass and a single, undergrown twig of a tree in the middle, with none of the manicured shrubbery or fountains one might find in the center of a similar courtyard in Evanston. The amenities were worn—appliances that looked about thirty years old, windows covered with thick coats of paint that rattled when you touched them or when a strong wind blew, porcelain bathroom fixtures that were scratched and yellow from decades of use by dozens of tenants. The only furniture I could afford was a set of cast-offs from an old college acquaintance that included a loud, orange geometric sofa he called "the clown couch" and a card table and folding chairs I used as a dining room set. The back porch was the top of a rickety wooden staircase painted in industrial gray where, if you forgot to close the lid tight on your garbage can, rats the size of house cats could be found rummaging late at night.

But it was mine. There weren't two roommates or seven siblings with whom I had to share a bathroom or a bedroom or a phone. There was no one around to tell me I should quit acting and get a real job at a bank. There were no brass rings to compete with—no one could tell me I wasn't good enough to be there, unless I didn't pay the rent.

Because the moving fund I'd saved would only last me about two weeks, I headed downtown on the El after just a couple of days unpacking and looked for work. Capitalizing on the skills I'd picked up at a string of word processing jobs in New York, I registered with a temp agency and immediately got a one-day position at a public relations firm, which turned into a three-year gig once they figured out I was decent at writing press releases.

Headshots in hand, I also headed into the offices of the three talent agents in town who would consider you for casting calls without an exclusive representation agreement, which was the requirement in New York. I dropped off piles of photos and résumés at each of the three, and though the majority of work for which they sought talent consisted of print ads and "bite and smile" TV commercials for things like granola bars and potato chips, the residuals could be lucrative, especially if it was a national spot. And, when the occasional call for a movie or television show came in, word was that an agency would be much more likely to send you if you'd already made them some money doing commercial work.

Patti, my friend and frequent scene partner from acting class at Northwestern, was working in Chicago theatre and met me one day at the Melrose Diner in Lakeview, one of Chicago's gayest neighborhoods. While an overabundance of cute guys strolled in and out of the Melrose, distracting me a little from Patti's lesson, she explained how Chicago worked as a theatre town. As in New York, Equity auditions were closed to actors who weren't part of the union. But Chicago also had a thriving non-Equity theatre scene, the equivalent of New York's Off-Off-Broadway. Virtually all of these theatres had open auditions and, unlike in New York, their shows were reviewed by the three major newspapers: the *Tribune*, the *Sun-Times*, and the *Reader*. Virtually every show that went up in Chicago received some form of press attention. This meant that a good performance, even if it was in a small, non-Equity house that seated thirty people and paid actors nothing, could get you a nice review that could later open much bigger doors.

Slightly daunting as it all seemed, it also seemed manageable. Instead of relying on blind faith, serendipity, and endless pavement pounding, as seemed to be required to get an acting career going in New York, an aspiring actor could come up with a workable plan. So I checked the *Reader* and the Non-Equity Hotline weekly for auditions. Once I saved up enough money from my job at the PR agency, I started taking voice lessons and dance and acting classes. And, as recommended, I checked in with my agents at least once a week. I put on the right clothes to look my castable best, took a late lunch from work, and stopped by each office, usually for no more than thirty seconds, just to remind them of my existence.

"Hi, Beth!" I'd say with my brightest toothpaste-commercial smile when I checked in at the Shirley Hamilton Agency on a Friday afternoon, standing at the four-foot reception counter that looked like one you might find at the Department of Motor Vehicles. Then, "Michael Sadowski checking in," to save both Beth and me the embarrassment of her trying to remember who I was.

"Hi, Michael. Nothing right now," Beth would say, smiling pleasantly but barely looking up from her desk.

"OK, thanks."

This was the usual length of my visits at Shirley Hamilton. At the Harrise Davidson Agency, the routine was more or less the same as it was at Shirley's, except the DMV-style fortress was replaced by a half door that allowed you to look into the agents' offices, but never go in.

"Hi, Michael. It's Don from Emelia's. I have an audition for you. Give me a call." Click.

These were the messages I waited for, checked my answering machine three and four times a day for, hoping that one day the big call would come. When I first registered with Emelia Lawrence Agency, Don, one of the agents there, took an interest in me, seemed to think I had potential. I heard from Don five or six times within the first three months, mostly for TV commercials and print ads. They weren't exactly my dream acting jobs, but after several years of beating my head against the theatrical wall in New York, they were gigs I would have given up my apartment to get.

I loved being on the list of actors Don would think of when a casting director called, and after a while I didn't even have to check in anymore because we were in frequent communication about real auditions. Then, when I didn't get any callbacks from casting directors, Don's calls tapered off. I started checking in every week again, and Don was cordial, but it was pretty clear he was starting to feel like he was wasting his time on me. Whereas at first Don would ask around the office when I stopped by to see if there was anything he might be able to send me out for, eventually it felt just like checking in at the other agencies:

"Hi, Don. Just checking in."

"Nothing right now."

My first theatrical job was in an Equity house as an "extra." The play took place on the floor of the Chicago Mercantile Exchange, and the theatre hired a bunch of nonunion actors at zero salary to shout out generic trades and pass around cards to create a hubbub on the trading floor while the principal characters (played by the paid Equity actors) exchanged the real, scripted dialogue.

My second theatre job was to replace an actor in a non-Equity show that had been running for a while and had thus already been reviewed. My third was in a musical that had also been running for several months, and I was in the ensemble—playing what my father would have called "one of the crowd"—not much of a chance to make a mark there. My fourth gig was as an understudy. It was in an Equity theatre, and the role was great, but since I never had the opportunity to go on, I couldn't use it as a credit on my résumé other than with the qualifier "understudy."

Three years in Chicago and I still had never been reviewed in one of the papers, still had not gotten a union card from Actors' Equity, still had not gotten any commercial work except for one nonunion extra spot in a fast-food commercial. In the highlight of my Chicago acting career to that point, I wore a tuxedo and waved at the camera from the back seat of a limousine, playing a member of a wedding party that ditches the reception to eat sliders at White Castle.

~

My life in Chicago finally took a dramatic turn not at a theatre or in a casting director's office but at a bookstore. Now gone, it was a small, independent bookseller in the neighborhood Chicago's gay community affectionately called Boystown, a name that later went mainstream and received official recognition by the mayor. I had been in Chicago for four years, and I'd recently adopted a new strategy of trolling bookstores in neighborhoods where I knew a lot of gay men lived. I was tired of meeting guys at bars, and I thought a bookstore might be a place to strike up a conversation with a cute guy about something more substantive than the latest Madonna or George Michael video.

Up to this point, I had slept with a lot of men in Chicago, probably two or three dozen if I'm really keeping track, the vast majority of whom I'd met at the bars. After work, it was TJ's, a garden-level hangout on fashionable Oak Street frequented by high-end hair stylists, department store employees, and the occasional business traveler staying in one of the nearby luxury hotels, which I saw the upper floors of on more than one occasion. On Sundays, it was Gentry, a piano bar where I sometimes sang open mic and could use a song as a come-on. On Saturday nights, it was the strip on Boystown's Halsted Street, where all evening I'd walk in and out of preppy Roscoe's, video-themed Sidetrack, and countless other places the names of which I don't remember. Each bar on Halsted had its own signature clientele—muscle jocks, pretty boys, bad boys, papa bears—none of which I ever felt I measured up to. (Gay men, I learned, flee from all sorts of masculinity images in their childhoods only to create their own as adults.) I'd circle each bar two and three times a night, hoping to see a new face or have someone on whom I'd fixed my gaze earlier in the evening gaze back.

The bars and the men I met there were, at least in part, consolation for the acting career I didn't have and for so much more I still couldn't name. They were a way out of the isolation of my empty apartment on the far North Side, which was starting to feel like my college dorm had on a Saturday night, desolate while the big party, or at least the one I imagined, was happening further downtown. I never went to the bars looking for sex—the void I felt ran much deeper than any one-night stand could fill. Yet despite starting these evenings with resolutions to the contrary, I almost always slept with guys the night I met them. After hours of searching for human connection, I couldn't resist the temptation—yes—of the physical presence of a man and the affirmation of being chosen but also of the promise of companionship, the hope that somehow a chance encounter might evolve into something that actually mattered.

Sometimes the bar boys would become boyfriends. They'd stay in the picture for two or three months if the conversation was easy, the sex was good, or—if I'm being honest—there was a car, a lake house, or a nice downtown apartment involved. Other times it would only last for one night. Anywhere from one to eight hours after our respective orgasms, we would exchange phone numbers (and, if we hadn't yet, last names), and then he wouldn't call, leaving me feeling either rejected or relieved depending on how our night together had gone. Most times, it lasted somewhere between a few days and a few weeks, what one of the guys I dated wearily referred to on our second night together as the "four-date dance card," after which both the sex and the conversation would start to lose its spark. I think I saw that guy twice after that. That time, I was the one who stopped calling.

⁓

On this particular night, I thought about stopping by the bookstore to see a cute, bespectacled clerk who looked like he'd been sent by one of my agents to audition for the role of Cute Bookstore Clerk in a commercial. I'd chatted with this guy at the register a few times and was starting to develop a crush on him, but I didn't know if I could ask him out. Was it proper to invite a guy on a date while he was ringing up your books?

What if he wasn't even gay? Yes, the bookstore was in Boystown, but it wasn't specifically a gay bookstore. One good thing about the bars was that at least there, the rules were clear. But as the July sun started to set, and I faced the prospect of another night walking up and down Halsted Street, in and out of Roscoe's and Sidetrack looking for love, I wondered what I had to lose. The worst that could happen if the cute clerk said no was that I would have to find another bookstore to try and pick up smart guys.

When I finally walked into the store, I was crestfallen to see someone other than my crush behind the counter. I peeked around the stacks to see if maybe he was helping a customer or stocking books, then I distractedly flipped through a few pages of some gay-themed novels to make it look like I had actually come in to buy a book. Once it was clear that the object of my affection wasn't working that night, I headed for the door, still not sure if I would hit the bars or just go home and watch the episodes of *One Life to Live* I'd saved up on my VCR. Then:

"Hey, Maahchael!"

A thick Texas accent rang out from one of the aisles. It was Sean, a guy who had worked as stage manager on the non-Equity musical I'd been in the ensemble of a year or two before. Sean was a sweet guy, and we had a lot of laughs working together on the show, but he wasn't really my type. Standing next to Sean, however, was a bookishly handsome young man he introduced to me as Daniel Fuller, who could just as easily have been sent on the Cute Bookstore Clerk audition as the guy who actually worked at the bookstore.

Daniel had tortoise shell glasses and a thick head of medium brown hair that looked effortlessly wavy in all the right ways. He was a little shorter than me, maybe five-foot-nine to my five-foot-eleven, but he was compactly well-built, as the way he filled out his T-shirt made clear. As the three of us chatted, it was hard not to stare into his wide brown eyes. Sean enthusiastically explained that Daniel was an actor, which he seemed to think might interest me but was actually a turnoff. (The last thing an actor needs in a boyfriend is another actor.) Unlike me, though, Daniel seemed to be having a modicum of success getting work and was currently playing the hapless husband in a screwball farce that was running in town. (Another turnoff: the only thing worse than having another actor as a boyfriend is having one who has a better career than you.)

"So, what are you looking for in here?" Daniel asked to make conversation.

"Oh—" I stumbled for a second, obviously not wanting to say it was the cute salesclerk who wasn't on duty that night. "I was just looking at the latest Armistead Maupin."

"Oh, I *loved* it. *Sure of You*," he said wistfully. "So sweet. I've read them all."

A man who reads. Actor or not, now I was a goner.

But Sean was there, and though it seemed like he was trying to make a love connection between Daniel and me, I was never good at figuring these things out for sure. So after a few minutes, we just said polite goodbyes and I headed back to Rogers Park.

Riding the El on the way home, I was tingling from the way Daniel and I had looked at one another, or at least the way I'd looked at him, and I wondered if I should look him up in the phonebook when I got home. There might be a lot of Daniel Fullers, I thought. What if I called the wrong one? What if he was unlisted? Or, what if he and Sean were a couple? It didn't seem like it at the bookstore, but that would have been terrible, especially considering the way Daniel and I had seemed to be flirting. And could I even assume that Daniel was gay? (Then again, the chances that a straight man would read Armistead Maupin's entire *Tales of the City* series were pretty slim.)

About twenty minutes after my arrival home, while I was still deliberating over whether or not to look up Daniel's number, the phone rang.

"Hi, Michael. It's Daniel Fuller," he began slowly and sheepishly, as if it were a little scandalous to call up a guy you had just met in a bookstore an hour before. "We met at the bookstore earlier?"

Yeah. I remembered. (I had never felt more grateful for my listing in the Chicago white pages.)

"Oh—hey, Daniel!" I said casually, realizing I could play it a little cool because it was already pretty clear what this phone call was about. "It was nice to meet you. And it was so good to see Sean, too. He's great. I haven't seen him in so long."

"I was wondering—" Daniel said, sounding like he was shrugging his shoulders on the opposite end of the phone line. "I don't know—if you might want to go out for dinner or a drink sometime?"

Already hypnotized by the sound of his phone voice, which was deep, soft, and just a little far away, I answered with perfect composure, "Yes. I think that would be very nice."

~

As a working actor, Daniel's weekend evenings were tied up with performances, so I met him at the theatre the following Saturday night after one of his shows. Once he took off his costume and makeup, we walked back to his apartment in Lakeview. As we chatted a little awkwardly—about the play he was in, about the unusually cool summer evening—I realized it was already close to midnight. The streets were emptying, most people were going home, and our evening was just getting started. Was there any doubt where this night was headed?

At Daniel's apartment, we sat on the living room floor, shared some wine, and talked for an hour, maybe two, about things that would have been met with blank stares had I brought them up with most of the guys I met in bars. We talked politics, literature, queer culture. As a conversationalist, Daniel was a little hard to keep up with. He was knowledgeable, well read, with an eclectic taste in music that went far beyond the mostly top-forty repertoire I could sing word for word. But he seemed to view me as his intellectual peer, and this fact tipped the balance even more decisively in his favor. An hour into our first date, I was already falling hard for this guy.

Of course, Daniel and I spent that night in his bed, and I understood for the first time how sexual desire can fuse with intellectual connection and intense emotion into one feeling, with one person. (In other words, the sex was so incredible it didn't even feel like sex.) The next morning, we went out for breakfast at a diner in his neighborhood. My whole body buzzed as we held hands across the table, a broad-daylight, public declaration of the fact that Daniel and I were already well on our way to becoming a couple.

Over the next few weeks, we became official boyfriends: talking every day on the phone, not making plans with friends until we knew what the other was doing, sleeping at one another's apartments on the weekends. I shared the news with Patti on the phone one night.

"Oh!" she said, sounding a little taken aback. Then, cautiously: "I actually know Daniel. That's . . . great. Just . . ." She stopped midsentence.

"Just what?"

"I don't know. Just be careful, honey. Watch your heart."

"Yes, of course I will. I always do," I said. But then I realized there was something more in what Patti was saying than a general advisory not to take romance too lightly. I'd acted in a lot of scenes with Patti, and I knew when she was playing subtext.

"What exactly are you saying?" I asked.

"Nothing . . . just. Well . . . I've been here in town doing theatre a little longer than you. Daniel's dated a few people I know, and . . . let's just say it didn't always end well."

"What do you mean? What happened?"

Patti clearly didn't want to go any further now, but it was too late for her to turn back.

"Nothing terrible, it's just . . . well, he's broken a few hearts, that's all. Listen, just forget I said anything. If it's going great and he treats you right, go for it. Just be careful."

What Patti said rattled me a little, so I started watching Daniel for signs. Was he losing interest? Was he slow to return my phone calls? Was there any way he could be seeing someone else when he wasn't with me? None of it seemed to be happening. Besides, who hadn't broken someone's heart at least once, somewhere along the line? I knew I had. And even if Daniel had done so multiple times, maybe he had good reasons for it. There are two sides to every breakup story.

One night about five weeks into our relationship, Daniel was dropping me off in front of the Ann Sather restaurant on Belmont Avenue, where I was meeting a friend for dinner while Daniel headed off for his call at the theatre. We had already said goodbye, and I was halfway out of his car, when he called out to me:

"Wait—don't go yet. I need to tell you something."

"Sure . . ." I said, sitting back down into the car, a little tentatively.

Daniel sighed from what sounded like the depth of his soul. Then, with a tone in his voice I'd never quite heard before, he said, intensely yet almost in a whisper, "Michael Sadowski—I love you. *God*, I love you."

Stunned, I looked over and took in the image of Daniel sitting in the driver's seat, which was different from the way I had ever seen anyone else look in a driver's seat before. His face glowed with a joy so deep, it almost looked like sadness. His emotions seemed to pulse through his entire body, then catch in his throat when he tried to put them into words. As Daniel's silver Honda Civic idled along the curb on Belmont Avenue, I saw something I had been waiting to see my entire life: someone who was deeply and completely happy—or, more to the point, deeply and completely happy because of me.

"I love you, Daniel Fuller," I said, from my own place of quiet, intense, reverent joy. We didn't kiss or even take each other's hands. We just looked at one another, long and hard, our bodies both twitching from an electricity that couldn't channel itself through mere physical expression. I got out of the car and felt the setting Chicago sun warm me in a way I hadn't in all of my four years there.

∼

After the l-word, Daniel and I were all in, our emotions reeling in a heady new world. The next thing Daniel wanted to do, he said, was bring me home for Thanksgiving to meet his parents, something he had never done with any of his previous boyfriends. Home was La Jolla, California, where Daniel's father was a physics professor at UC–San Diego. As uncomfortable as it made me to have Daniel's parents buy me a plane ticket—my own father had never even bought me one—it was starting to look like we were all going to be family soon.

Then one night, a few weeks after the Thanksgiving plan was made, I was lying awake in Daniel's apartment, staring into the dark while he slept peacefully beside me. Increasingly, Daniel had been keeping to his side of the bed, barely touching me for the six or seven hours we slept, whereas before it had been spooning all night. Having endured a few weeks of what felt like an expanding gulf between us—and my wondering what was wrong with him or with me—I literally took matters into my own hands. Following many minutes of nervous deliberation, I reached over and held him. I hoped he would hold me back or at least allow himself to be held, lean in to the old feeling of us. Still asleep, he pulled away and, unable to spend another night together yet alone, I woke him up.

"Daniel?"

"Huh?"

"Can I talk to you for a minute?"

"OK," he said, starting to wake up a little. "Is everything OK?"

"Yeah. I guess. Actually, I don't know."

Did I really want to do this?

"What's going on?" he asked, half sounding like he was confused and really wanted to know and half sounding like he was annoyed that I had woken him up in the middle of the night.

Choosing words I had rehearsed for days, I then chronicled all the little shifts I'd noticed in the previous few weeks that were starting to add up.

"I feel like something's changed, not just in bed but in a lot of things," I said. "And I'm scared we're growing apart."

"OK," Daniel answered, a little wider awake now.

"I don't know what it is. It just feels different between us lately. Like, sometimes you sound annoyed when I call you in the morning, and you never used to before. Or you always say you're tired when I ask you up to my apartment. You haven't been there in weeks. Or when I try to hold your hand, sometimes you pull away. And you seem in your own world a lot of the time—like I'm talking to you and you're somewhere else. I don't know. I don't know."

After hearing myself recount things that, when spoken out loud, sounded insignificant, ridiculous even, I wondered if I'd been rambling, if I'd said too much, if what I'd said were even true. Maybe it was all just insecurity, neediness on my part instead of an accurate perception of reality. I'd woken my boyfriend up in the middle of the night to talk about *us*? To talk about my *feelings*? What was happening to me? Was I becoming *clingy*?

"Maybe it's just me," I equivocated. "Maybe I'm overanalyzing. Maybe I want too much. I don't know. I don't know. It just—feels different."

Daniel straightened, swung around, sat on the edge of the bed, and sighed. Then, seemingly out of nowhere, he started to cry. There was in fact a problem, he said. He'd struggled with it a lot over the years and referred to it, over and over in what eventually became a tearful monologue, as a fear of intimacy.

"I have this damn fear of intimacy thing," he said through his tears. "I just have never been able to get close to people. I don't know what it is, really. I don't know what's wrong with me. It's like I'm terrified—or something, I don't know. I push people away. Like I'm trapped by my own emotions."

Stunned and rendered silent, I listened while Daniel's crying gave way to several minutes of full-on sobbing.

"I *hate* this thing, this—this fear of intimacy thing," he moaned, barely choking the words out. "But I don't know what to do. I just don't know what I can do. It's awful. It's just awful!"

"Fear of intimacy," I finally said back slowly, repeating the name of this psychological wedge that I'd just learned had come between us. "I—I don't think I know what that means."

It probably sounded callous to Daniel, but I really *didn't* know—I couldn't understand what he was saying. I'd never heard of a fear of intimacy as a real condition before, and it didn't make any sense to me, especially since Daniel was the one who had moved our relationship to the "I love you" stage just a few weeks earlier. I wanted to understand. I wanted Daniel to tell me more. I wanted this conversation to make us closer. Maybe by talking about his fear of intimacy we could become *more* intimate and beat this thing. But now I felt even more as if I weren't in the room. All Daniel seemed able to do was sob and provide one-word answers to my questions.

Was it the l-word that had triggered this, I asked?

Maybe.

Was this a pattern with other guys he'd had relationships with?

Yes.

Did it have anything to do with Graham, the bad-boy type I'd seen him flirting with a few weeks earlier when we were out with a bunch of people from his show?

No.

But I still wondered.

I tried to be sympathetic, especially given how emotionally paralyzed all this seemed to make him. I tried not to take it personally. At the same time, I couldn't help viewing the situation through my own psychological kaleidoscope of isolation, fear of abandonment, and the messages of worthlessness I'd started hearing again as soon as Daniel had started pulling back. And I couldn't help wondering: did I have a boyfriend with a real problem we could work through, or was it just the four-date dance card playing itself out again, except this time over four months? Was Daniel's condition real or was it just a self-diagnosed excuse to do what he really wanted to do: leave me and move on to someone else? Was this Daniel the actor's greatest performance? I didn't know. All I knew was that what Patti had said was starting to make a lot of sense.

Once Daniel stopped crying and lay back down on the bed, I thought about reaching out and holding him until he fell asleep. I still wanted to, but I didn't. I just wasn't sure if I was allowed do that anymore.

~

Following Daniel's midnight confession, things limped along pretty much as they had in the previous few weeks. Then there was the matter of the nonrefundable plane ticket to California.

As if having Daniel's parents buy me an expensive flight hadn't already felt strange, going on the trip while Daniel and I were in this brittle state felt even stranger. But canceling the trip seemed the worst option of all, and since Daniel never suggested it, neither did I. That would have been the final gesture, confirmation of the fact that we were done as a couple, and I still held on to hope that things could turn around. Maybe the Thanksgiving trip would be just what we needed. I could charm Daniel with how good I was with his little nephew. Or maybe his mother would love me—mothers always did—and that would seal the deal. So, fear of intimacy and all, I boarded a plane to San Diego the day before Thanksgiving to meet the folks.

"Debra Fuller!" said his mother heartily, hand outstretched, when we rendezvoused at baggage claim. Debra was a tall, athletic looking woman, tanned and trim in just the way I had expected a sixty-year-old, well-off Southern California woman to be. Daniel's father, James, was shorter, gray-haired, and a little mussed up, in just the way I expected a university physics professor to be.

It was immediately obvious from Debra's and James's demeanors at the airport that Daniel hadn't told them anything about his fear of intimacy, or at least how it was affecting the two of us. And I had no sense of whether that would make the weekend better or worse.

"It'll be so nice for you to finally meet the rest of the family tomorrow," Debra said. "Everyone's really looking forward to it. They've heard so much about you!"

Apparently, as far as Debra was concerned, I was already the new son-in-law. All that was left was for Daniel and me to pick out a china pattern.

It was a chatty, cordial ride from the airport in James's leather-seated luxury sedan, mostly small talk about the flight and the plans for the weekend, with the dark of the car easing the conversation until the inevitable arrival at the Fuller home. Before we even parked the car at the house in La Jolla, I learned it was just one of three residences the family owned, an oceanside property near Pebble Beach and another place in Palm Springs being the other two.

"James and I might head out to Palm Springs on Friday," Debra tossed off casually from the passenger seat. "You guys could come with us, or you could have the whole house in La Jolla to yourself—it's up to you. We can play it by ear, I guess."

The La Jolla house was so big it had a name: Seven Palms. It was an adobe-style mansion with a huge in-ground swimming pool in the back, a center courtyard with a fountain, and a formal living room I never saw anyone sit in because there were so many other places in the house to congregate. Yet despite all its California-style opulence, the house had no heat. Most of the time, the Fullers explained, this wasn't a problem, but the area was experiencing an unusual Thanksgiving cold snap. They apologized for the bedroom Daniel and I were to share, which was still cold despite the formidably sized space heater they'd set up. Secretly, I was glad for the chill, since I thought it might be a reason for Daniel and me to keep each other warm under the covers.

"I'm tired, and it's just weird with my parents in the house," Daniel said when I tried to initiate sex on our first night in California. This struck me as odd considering how welcoming Debra and James had both been toward me and the fact that the house was so big, they couldn't possibly have heard us. But Daniel was clearly not in the mood, so I rolled over to the other side of the bed and resigned myself to the cold.

I don't remember much about the rest of our time in La Jolla. I vaguely recall an uncomfortable Thanksgiving dinner where I met the family—brother, sister, nieces, nephews. I remember Daniel's taking me into Nordstrom and showing me a sweater he said he would have bought for my birthday, which was coming up in a few days, if only he could have afforded it. I remember a walk through a nature preserve in which Daniel and I had the most intimate conversation we'd had in a long time. Daniel talked about how much he had struggled in his life to find inner peace, and though I wasn't completely sure what he meant by this, I told him that I'd wrestled with similar feelings myself. (Hadn't I?) Maybe, I allowed myself to hope, we could try to find inner peace together, whatever that meant to him. But the more Daniel talked about his emotional demons and his efforts to vanquish them, the clearer it became that he saw his quest for peace as a solo journey, one that didn't include me.

On Saturday morning, with Debra and James having gone to Palm Springs, I left Daniel alone at the Fuller house and rented a car. It wasn't a complete change of plans. I had told Daniel before we left Chicago, once things started to go south between us and I thought I might need an escape route, that I'd probably take a day over the Thanksgiving weekend to visit my friend Robin, who now lived in Los Angeles. Daniel didn't seem to mind, said he had a lot of errands to run that day. The part we hadn't planned was that, after my day in LA, I wouldn't return to La Jolla for the flight home.

"I called United, and they let me change my ticket from San Diego to LAX," I said when I called Daniel Saturday afternoon, after a pep talk from Robin over lunch had strengthened my resolve. "So I'm just going to stay overnight in LA and then leave from here. It makes more sense instead of coming all the way back down there."

"Oh!" Daniel said, sounding surprised and a little hurt—just as I had intended.

Then I added, sincerely and with a little bit of sadness, "And your parents are great. Please tell them when they get back that I said thank you for everything."

"Oh—sure. I will." Daniel said, still sounding shell-shocked, but maybe a little relieved, too.

I called Daniel from my apartment in Chicago the night I flew back from LA and he from San Diego. I knew exactly when his flight would arrive because I was supposed to have been on it myself, had marked it on my calendar and anticipated it for weeks. I calculated the amount of time it would have taken him to drive from the airport and called just when I figured he would be walking through the door to his apartment.

"So—" I asked, after all the awkward "how was your flight?" pleasantries had been exchanged. "What happens now?"

"I don't know," he sighed, then grew silent. It was clear that I was going to have to do the heavy lifting.

"Well—I don't really think I can do this anymore, not if it's going to be like this," I said. "Maybe we shouldn't see each other for a while or something. I don't know. I just don't know what more I can do."

"Yeah, I know, I know," Daniel said blankly, the soft, far-off timbre of his phone voice, which had once melted me, now the sound of real distance.

"So—I guess that's it?" I both said and asked, trying to jumpstart a breakup to which Daniel still seemed unwilling to commit.

Even at that point, had Daniel offered me the slightest crumb, I would have come right back to the table. But all he said was, "I don't know. I don't know what I think."

We said goodbye and hung up, still not having made a firm decision about anything.

The next day was my birthday, so I waited for the phone to ring instead of picking it up myself. Even if it was just going to be the continuation of our breakup conversation, I wanted Daniel to call, to let me know that I still mattered to him. He didn't. I wondered if it even crossed his mind.

～

The months after Daniel and I broke up—or, more accurately, faded out—were as dark as those I had experienced at Northwestern, maybe even darker. Except instead of heading out to the rocks and contemplating dropping into Lake Michigan, I headed to the bars. I slept with even more men, woke up in strange apartments and hotel rooms, once without any recollection of what had happened the night before. I rarely did any drugs other than alcohol, but one night an out-of-towner brought me back to his hotel room at the Palmer House after we'd already had quite a bit to drink. He had poppers with him, an inhalable form of amyl nitrate that had once been extremely popular in gay clubs. I had no experience with poppers. They were pretty much out of fashion by this time, 1991, but I knew they had been a staple of the gay scene and it seemed prudish not to try to them, especially since I was already in this man's hotel room. (The time to express moral objection to anything had long since passed.) I don't remember anything from the rest of that night, only our conversation the next day, when he assured me in my morning-after panic that we hadn't done anything unsafe. He seemed like a nice, gentle guy, so I believed him. He gave me his phone number—with an area code from Cleveland or Pittsburgh or somewhere—but I was so embarrassed after having blacked out on alcohol and poppers that I never called.

Twice as a result of sleeping around, I contracted crabs, the discomfort, contagion, and self-disgust of which condemned me to celibacy for a few weeks. Then I headed right back out to the bars. By this point, I often *was* going out looking for sex, believing less and less that a supportive relationship with another man was even possible. Some thrilling, slightly dangerous man hunting and an orgasm could silence, at least for a few hours, the voices of worthlessness that now rang in my head at every moment I wasn't distracted by something else.

Besides the fact that I thought Daniel had found me inadequate as a lover and as a companion, I also couldn't help feeling that he had deemed me unworthy of the three-home California lifestyle his family enjoyed. I had come of age in the 1980s, when college students lived by the dictates of *The Preppy Handbook,* and had internalized the message— seared into my consciousness by the Phi Psi fraternity—that where you came from was who you were. It was no wonder, then, that Daniel ultimately distanced himself from me—the failed actor who grew up with a pigeon coop in his backyard (not that I ever told him about *that*)— because all I wanted now was to be rid of me, too.

This was also an era in which AIDS completely dominated the consciousness of gay men. I'd known at least a dozen people who were dead and knew many more who were sick or positive, including Paul, my ex-boyfriend in New York, who would die several years later. In 1991, a positive HIV test was still a death sentence. It was years before we would hear about drug cocktails that could make the disease a chronic, manageable illness. I was strangely fortunate in that, as a late-blooming gay male, I had never known a sexual world without AIDS, and this knowledge influenced my behaviors almost all the time. Still, I'd had a few experiences early on, including one with Paul, that had fallen into the "possibly unsafe" category, and these factored into the constant calculations I made about the likelihood of my getting sick. Sometimes I'd assure myself that it was getting close to the seven-year window that doctors were saying was the incubation period for the virus, so I was probably OK. Other times, I'd sit in my empty apartment and the calculations clicking away in my head would evolve into full-blown AIDS panic, convincing me I would die a slow, lonely death that people would say I deserved. (The Christian right was in its heyday during this era, too.) The sheer terror of it all kept me from getting tested, which of course would have been the smart and responsible thing to do. Eventually, the seven-year window after I'd been with Paul elapsed, just in time for news stories to come out that were now saying things like, "The virus can remain dormant for up to fifteen years."

Still, none of this kept me from the bars. As the weeks went by, I shifted my strategy from one bar to the next, holding on to a vague hope that if I could just find the right crowd, I might find the right guy, one who would stay around, and whom I might want to stay around, for longer than one night. After exhausting the Halsted Street strip, I started hanging out at Berlin, a bar near the Belmont El tracks that attracted a slightly edgy, alternative type of guy I thought might have a little more depth. (The music was Depeche Mode and The Cure instead of Madonna and Whitney Houston.) I met a guy at Berlin one night who was cute and smart. We went to his apartment. I remember to this day his first and last name, with the initials DR, which he wrote above his phone number on the inside flap of a pack of matches we'd picked up on the bar. I called him the next day and he never called back.

I went back to Berlin a week or two after that, hoping I might run into DR. Maybe his face would burst into a spontaneous smile. Maybe he would tell me he had inadvertently erased my message and was thrilled to see me again. But the place was packed on this particular night, even more so than usual, full of spiky-haired gay men and the pink-haired women who loved them. And while at first it seemed in this huge crowd that there had to be someone worth meeting, even if I never found DR, it was impossible to get a good look at anyone's face much less have a conversation given the din and density of the crowd. I pushed my way through to the bar to get a drink, scanning faces as I went, then to the bathroom, scanning more faces, then back to the bar, still looking for DR or, eventually, any viable replacement for him. I repeated this bar-to-bathroom, back-and-forth routine a few more times, trying to look purposeful, like someone with a destination instead of the desperate soul looking for love that I was. Eventually, I couldn't bring myself to say "excuse me" one more time, and I headed for the El to go home.

It was an especially cold night, and it took especially long for the northbound train to show up to take me back to Rogers Park. As I waited for the El in the biting wind, I huddled with other desperate Chicagoans under the inadequate glow of the overhead heat lamp. I was probably a little more impervious to the cold than most for the sheer number of gin and tonics I'd downed going back and forth to the bar at Berlin, but the wait was still frigid and miserable in the way only a late-night wait on a Chicago El platform can be. Finally, the northbound train pulled in and I got on, deeply grateful for its warmth and for the available empty seat, where I could curl up until Morse Avenue, the stop closest to my apartment.

The next thing I remember is waking up underground, at the Washington Street subway station. Washington Street is *south* of Belmont Avenue. When I opened my eyes and saw the sign for Washington, I bolted out of my seat, exited the train just as the doors were about to close, and headed up the dank subway stairwell out onto the street. I checked my watch. It was nearly three in the morning, easily two hours after I'd left Berlin. Having been pickpocketed on an El platform once before, I reached for my wallet and, to my great relief, it was still there. Not trusting myself enough to get back on the train, which was probably running at forty-minute intervals by this time of night anyway, I rifled through my wad of singles and fives. I prayed that I still had enough cash, after wasting so much of it at Berlin, for a cab back to the far North Side, and that I would be able to find one. Soon a driver pulled up and, seeming to sense my desperation, agreed to take me to Rogers Park for the amount of money I had left, about seventeen dollars.

As the taxi headed north on Lake Shore Drive and the lights of downtown Chicago receded behind me, I pieced together what must have happened. I had fallen asleep, traveled on the northbound train past my stop at Morse, all the way up to the red line's endpoint, Howard Street. Unnoticed by the train crew, or perhaps written off as a person who actually wanted to sleep on the El, I rode back into the trainyard and slept there until the train headed south again. I passed Morse a second time, then passed Belmont, where I'd gotten on in the first place. Two stops later, the train went underground, and I cruised along until some internal alarm clock kicked in at Washington, deep into the Chicago loop, probably the last stop on the line from which I could find a street cab at 3 a.m.

The next morning, as the gray winter light began peeking through the windows of my apartment, I felt grateful for the comfort and warmth the place had offered me at the end of my long, ridiculous journey. But

I also saw now that something there was slowly killing me. I didn't know what it was, only that if I didn't escape it, I wouldn't survive much longer.

I had been taking so many chances lately. Wasn't it just a matter of time before my luck ran out? Before I went home with the wrong stranger or had another sexual encounter, this time a fatal one, that I didn't remember the next morning? And now I had slept on the El with no awareness of where I was, a sitting duck for any mugger, pickpocket, or worse. Just like my father had done so many times, I'd had too much to drink and then stumbled through the dark trying to find my way home.

That morning, I decided I was leaving Chicago.

16

Tin Man

One morning in August of that same year, the phone rang early. It was 7:15, 7, maybe even 6:45. Although it was a Saturday, I was already awake clearing out cabinets and drawers, anxious for my move back to New York, now just three weeks away.

Unlike prior moves, which had snuck up on me and forced me to throw away everything I couldn't jam into a duffel bag, I approached this one like the pushing-thirty adult I now was, with months of preparation. The boxes piling up in the apartment were a welcome, daily reminder that I would soon leave Chicago behind, just as I had left behind so many other places, as if I still believed some other, better life might be waiting for me over the rainbow.

For the previous two years, I'd been part of a theatre company that performed a musical called *The Wizard of AIDS* on college campuses and at high schools and community centers around the Midwest. The show is a parody of *The Wizard of Oz* in which Dorothy and her three male sidekicks learn how to prevent HIV transmission while hounded by the Wicked Witch of Unsafe Sex, who is killed in the show's climax by a giant condom (portrayed by a Hefty bag). I played the Tin Man, heartless, living in fear of an STD, and rusting in his own secluded corner of the forest until Dorothy convinces him to follow the yellow brick road and he learns from the wizard how to trust love again.

Traveling with *The Wizard of AIDS*, I made the kind of friendships you can only make on the road. My fellow cast members and I shared stories, sang folk songs, confessed deep secrets in the company van while driving the interstates of Illinois, Indiana, and Wisconsin late into the night. But it all came too late to keep me in Chicago. Once a tour was over and I returned to the silence of my empty apartment, the voices that reminded me of all my failures and failings were there, waiting for me. I knew my only chance to get away from them was to leave, though I also knew I was running out of places to hide.

New York was, admittedly, a strange choice of destination. Hadn't I just fled from there five years earlier? What did I think I was going to find that hadn't been there before? I had no job waiting for me, no plan for earning money once I got to town. There was an acting teacher in Manhattan I'd read about and was vaguely interested in studying with. Maybe, I thought, he could finally crack open the lock on my emotions that had been jammed shut for so long. But I also wondered if I even wanted to continue pursuing an acting career. I would be turning thirty soon. Maybe it was time I started on another road before it was too late.

I didn't expect the proximity of New York to my family to make much of a difference. Except for a few oblique statements I'd made to Kathy one night over the phone when my despair over Daniel was impossible to hide, I still hadn't told any of my siblings—Benny's and my tacit understanding aside—that I was gay. Benny's experience with coming out twelve years earlier had served as a cautionary tale and is, for the most part, not my story to tell. But when Benny left Brown and transferred to Columbia so that he could be closer to his then-boyfriend, Tim, he returned for a time to New Jersey. He came out to our siblings then, years later reporting to me that "it didn't go well." He recounted tearful conversations, a family meeting in which they tried to convince him he wasn't really "that way," and his ultimate—and very rational—decision to just clam up, stop talking about it, and eventually move to Atlanta when Tim's employer transferred him there. It was twelve years later now, but despite how immutable being gay felt to me—and how centrally it defined me not only sexually and emotionally but politically, too—I still lived a huge part of my life in the closet. When it came to my sisters, my brothers, and especially my father, the closet still felt like the only safe place.

After I moved to Chicago, I checked in over the phone with one or another of my sisters every few weeks, gave them newsy updates in which I inflated my theatrical prospects and invariably said everything was fine. I performed a sort of ventriloquist act in these conversations, throwing a false voice to a character I manipulated while covering my own:

"Yeah, everything's good. It's really cold. Yeah, I have an audition next week for a commercial. My agent thinks I have a good chance. Who knows? We'll see what happens."

I had thought briefly about moving to the West Coast, as I'd planned to do upon graduating from college. But I was twenty-nine now, not twenty-one, old enough to realize that a move out west, where I had no connections and even fewer prospects than I had in New York, would get me nowhere. At least in New York, I had a few friends who could serve as an anchor for my umpteenth new life. Gerri and I were close again. We had talked a lot by phone in the previous few years—me confessing my heartbreak over Daniel and all the self-degradation that came with it, her confessing how the "brass ring" dream of her cohabitation with Paul had devolved into a tarnished, bottle-smashing nightmare when his alcoholism hit rock bottom. Patti was also in New York now, having been accepted to Columbia Law School, and was urging me to come back. So New York seemed to make sense, or at least more sense, than any alternative.

I called Blair, yet another former Northwestern classmate, who always seemed to have a room available in the rent-controlled Hell's Kitchen apartment he'd held onto since graduation. Sure enough, Blair's current roommate was leaving at the end of the summer. Meanwhile, Greg, one of my *Wizard of AIDS* castmates, was moving to Boston with his partner, Randy. So we made a plan. On Labor Day weekend, Greg, Randy, and I would rent a U-Haul, and they would drop me off at Blair's place en route to Boston. The apartment, the date, the truck—everything for my new life was set. And I wasn't about to let anything screw it up.

⁓

I knew exactly which phone call this was. Maybe it was the early hour. Maybe it was the calls that had come before. Maybe it was the fact that it was August 10, the forty-fifth birthday of my parents' first-born child, George. Maybe it was all of these things put together.

"I just wanted to tell you that Daddy died this morning," Donna said matter-of-factly on the other end of the line. She said it flatly, like it was a piece of neighborhood news she'd almost forgotten about. *So and so is pregnant. Such and such family is moving to Virginia. Oh, and our father died.*

"When?" I asked, even more matter-of-factly, as if time of death were the important fact to be gleaned from this conversation.

"Around five o'clock this morning," she said, her voice starting to break a little, sounding a little less matter-of-fact than she had before.

Yosh had been diagnosed with advanced brain cancer about two months earlier. For a long time, Elaine and my sisters missed the symptoms—the slurred speech, drooping eyelids, lack of balance, inability to walk in a straight line. After all, this was Yosh. These were all things we had seen for decades, so everyone's first assumption was that he was now getting smashed at all hours of the day and night. My sisters and Elaine chastised him for backsliding, having checked him into live-in rehab a year or two earlier when things had gotten really bad. Eventually, though, they figured out Yosh wasn't just getting drunk all day.

After the diagnosis, Yosh was admitted to Somerset Medical Center, the hospital four blocks from Lincoln Avenue where all of us had been born and where my mother had died, and he never left. My sisters visited him in shifts, then took the elevator to the floor where Aunt Helen was also dying, in her case of stage-four breast cancer. My sisters told me all this in our phone calls during my last few months in Chicago, while I continued to tell them everything was great on my end.

"I don't know exactly when the funeral is yet, but you might want to start calling the airlines," Donna suggested. "They have something called a bereavement fare, like a discount when there's a death in the family. I think that's what Benny's doing."

"Okay," I said, my voice flatlining even more than hers had at the beginning of the call. "I'll look into it."

What I didn't tell Donna was that I had already made up my mind. I wasn't going to Yosh's funeral, especially if he died while I was still living in Chicago.

"Okay, well, just let me know so we can have somebody pick you up," Donna said. "Call me later."

I had started the mental accounting weeks earlier. As soon as I heard Yosh's diagnosis, I created a balance sheet in my head, calculated how all the items added up. And the way I figured it, I could trace back just about everything that was wrong with my life, and everything that had always been wrong with it before, to Yosh.

First, there was his negligence throughout my childhood, his choice of booze over fatherhood, and his resulting inability to support me in anything where I might have remotely picked up any kind of masculinity skills. Wasn't this, at the core, the reason why I got harassed so much in elementary school, and then middle school, and then high school, and then even college? Wasn't this the reason why, whether I would actually grow up to be gay or not, I ended up being everyone's faggot?

Then there was my mother, and everything on the balance sheet associated with her: the way he'd pushed her, shoved her, cursed her, abandoned her, left her to fend for herself with eight kids while he was out "socializing" and probably cheating on her. And that thing he'd said in our driveway just days before she died, which still reverberated in my head. If it weren't for Yosh, I wondered, might my mother even still be alive?

Then there were all his bad choices, beyond the drinking. Maybe if he had at least finished high school, I might have been able to fit in better in college, instead of being the isolated fraternity reject I was. Maybe even Daniel, somehow, would have thought of me differently, as someone worth fighting for, fear of intimacy or not.

Finally, there was my sexuality. Despite the fact that I had never come out to my father, I felt his rejection preemptively, as acutely as if I had. As all his exhortations to go out for football had made blatantly clear, he had never simply accepted me as I was. Yet I was supposed to change all my plans, lose at least three days of income and packing time, and spend half of everything I'd saved for the move just to, as he used to say when someone died, "pay my respects"? The whole thing seemed—and really was—wildly illogical.

~

That afternoon I was at O'Hare Airport. My body felt like an empty cavity, devoid of all feeling except the buzz from the entire pot of coffee I'd drunk on an empty stomach. Feeling neither emotion nor volition, I wandered zombie-like through the motions of baggage check, security, and boarding. I paid no attention at all to the sensation of takeoff as I stared out the tiny window of a plane bound for Newark. All I thought about was what I was going to do once I got there. Yes, I was about to touch down on New Jersey tarmac, but I still hadn't surrendered. I still could just visit my brothers and sisters, help them through their grief, maybe show up for the post-funeral repast, then head back to Chicago. I didn't just have a move to prepare for—I had a score to settle.

Somewhere in midflight, maybe over Ohio or Pennsylvania, I realized that just as I hadn't had the nerve to sit the whole thing out in Chicago, I wasn't going to boycott the funeral once I got to New Jersey either. So I tried to picture myself at the wake, at the church, at graveside, and I finally felt something akin to an emotion as a wave of anxious dread moved through my body. How could I behave in a way that didn't feel like hypocrisy, like a betrayal of everything that had happened, of everything my father had put all of us through for so many years? Would it upset my siblings and my aunts and uncles if I didn't cry, didn't play the role of bereaved son, as they would obviously be expecting me to do? Did I care? I knew I couldn't fake it. How was I going to get through it all?

～

I don't remember landing, being picked up at the airport, or much else about my arrival in New Jersey. Yosh had sold the house on Lincoln Avenue a few years earlier and had moved in with Elaine, so I stayed with Donna and Steve through the wake and the funeral.

Donna and I sat up late in our pajamas the night I flew in. With the eleven o'clock news muted in the corner of her den, we opened a bottle of wine and she filled me in on the details of the previous few months. Yosh's cancer had originated in the brain, she said; it hadn't metastasized from some other part of his body. As Yosh got sicker, he became increasingly belligerent and verbally abusive to my sisters when they visited him, a manifestation of the disease, the doctors said. In essence, Yosh started talking to my sisters the way he had talked to my mother years before. They endured it, Donna said, because they had to and because they knew it was the cancer talking and not really their father.

Then Donna explained what had happened with Aunt Helen. She had started pulling her hair out, became increasingly nervous and edgy, and no one could figure out why. Eventually, my sisters learned, it was because of the lumps she was starting to find in her breasts, which she told no one about for months and which left her too paralyzed with fear to go to a doctor. It wasn't until she'd grown thin, weak, and sallow—and had already pulled out so much of her hair that she had bald patches all over her scalp—that my sisters knew something more than anxiety was going on. Helping Helen with her clothes one day when she had become barely able to function, Donna discovered the tumors that were now visible all over Helen's body.

"It's been an interesting few months, lemme tell you," Donna said, looking deep into her glass of white zin. "I don't know how we got through it, and it's not over yet."

~

The first viewing was in the afternoon, at the same funeral home where we had all gathered for my mother seventeen years before. My aunts and uncles—minus Helen, who hadn't been told as she lay dying that my father was already gone—congregated in the entry hall and offered condolences to my siblings and me as we came in, momentarily stepping out of their own individual clouds of grief. Given the pained looks on their faces, I could tell it was not the time to make a bold statement or register in any way that I didn't really care that Yosh was dead. So I put on the expectedly somber face of the bereaved, made quiet conversation, and nodded. I politely thanked people when they said, "I'm so sorry about your father" and held myself back from saying, "I'm not."

Then, without any of the terror or hesitation I'd felt when my mother died, I entered the room where Yosh's body lay in an open casket. In my memory, it's the same room, configured in exactly the same way as when my mother's body was laid there. The image of my mother in her coffin, indelible to this day though my glimpse lasted for less than a second, had made excruciating but logical sense. So much of what I'd known of Sophie had consisted of her suffering that seeing her lying dead, as jarring as it was at that point in my life, seemed an unsurprising end to things, a sign of ultimate defeat and surrender to a life that had always seemed to be beating her. But the memories I had of Yosh were of carousing, yelling, threatening, laughing, daring, socializing, telling people off. In his own loud, liquored-up way, my father had been full of life. So the image of him lying silent in a coffin, asleep but without the fits and snores of the alcohol-induced slumber I'd seen so many times in my childhood, was different than any I'd ever had of him. It's a worn-out cliché, but he looked peaceful lying there, more peaceful than I'd ever seen him, his long, blustering journey through life now over.

For the rest of the afternoon, I alternated between sitting in one of the folding chairs in the viewing room and standing in the back of the room or in the entry hall, chatting with whatever guests arrived—neighbors, cousins, a few of my old high school friends and their parents who showed up. I politely expressed my appreciation for their condolences, then quickly moved the conversation on to other things—the weather, who had recently had a baby, the fact that I was moving back to New York in a few weeks. I was glad to be finding a way through Yosh's funeral that didn't make me feel like a sellout. A few times I glanced over at his coffin, surprised each time that he looked as quiet and still as he had before.

~

At the evening visiting hours, my Uncle Mike, who had flown in from Arizona, decided he wanted to gather Yosh's brothers and sons for a military salute in front of the casket. While we were growing up, Yosh had often told Benny, Thomas, and me tales of his jumping out of airplanes as a paratrooper, trying to inspire us with army scenes for which we had no frame of reference. Once, when I was about eight, he took us to Kupper Airport, a small helicopter port about fifteen minutes' drive from Lincoln Avenue. Somehow he got the man running it that day to allow us inside one of the planes, where he took us back in time and described what the whole experience was like.

"Your daddy used to jump outta planes like this," he said. "They'd open the door, just like that there one, and we'd—*pshew!*—hop right out."

"*You* jumped out of a plane like this?" I asked, making no effort to hide my skepticism.

"Yeah, and if you didn't open your parachute at just the right time, that was it! And when we landed, there was shootin' all around us."

Parachute or not, I couldn't imagine anyone having the nerve to jump out of a plane while it was in flight, let alone Yosh. And, given the way I'd seen my father career around the streets while driving, I had a hard time imagining him being entrusted with such a sensitive assignment, one that obviously required impeccable timing and precision. But on the numerous occasions I asked my mother, my older siblings, or one of my aunts or uncles about it, they corroborated Yosh's story and confirmed that this was in fact what my father had done in the war. He had parachuted out of planes, landed in active battlefields surrounded by gunfire, once into a frigid river that nearly gave him frostbite. He'd even fought in the Battle of the Bulge and earned a Bronze Star for it.

During our mini-lesson at the airport, the helicopter's controls and gauges fascinated me for a few seconds. They looked like a really complicated car dashboard, and I briefly imagined taking the wheel and driving the helicopter at full speed down the runway until it took flight. But mostly, I remember being bored by Yosh's paratrooper stories because it was army talk, the military being yet another male-centered arena of life that made me feel like a failure.

None of us saw much of Uncle Mike because he lived out west, but whenever he visited New Jersey he always took a special shine to me as his namesake. So I was the one he came to when he wanted to gather my brothers and uncles for the salute.

Given all the milling around that happens at a wake, it took me a good twenty minutes to let everyone know about the military display Uncle Mike was planning in front of my father's casket, and by then the idea had fizzled a bit. I don't think even half of them participated. Benny didn't. George didn't. Most people seemed to think the whole thing was corny, maybe more of an attempt on Uncle Mike's part to put on a show than to pay tribute to my father.

But Uncle Mike had specifically asked me, so I felt obligated to take part. While Uncle Mike's small unit of a half dozen or so soldiers stood in the formation he had choreographed, I stared at Yosh in his coffin. I thought for a few seconds about what little I remembered of his paratrooper stories and our trip to Kupper Airport. Then:

"Salute!" shouted Uncle Mike in abrupt military style. I raised my stiffened hand sideways to my forehead for the first and only time in my life, certain that I was doing it wrong and hoping no one was looking.

~

The morning of the burial, my siblings and I had first access to the casket. Before the other mourners came in, my older sisters and brothers each knelt in front of our father one by one. Some crossed themselves, others didn't. I don't know if they knelt in birth order, but that's the way I remember it: George, then Donna, Larry, Nancy, Kathy, Benny . . .

When it was my turn, I wondered if it was time to make my statement, just take a seat, allow everyone to stare for a minute and then explain why I didn't need this moment, why I didn't have to say goodbye. But as with so many other things I'd done in the previous few days,

I had no sense of conviction about this one either. I dutifully followed suit and walked slowly toward my father's body. Despite the fact that I never prayed and didn't believe in any kind of god, I knelt at the padded bar in front of his casket, automatically, spinelessly—again—just because it was what everyone else had done.

With my father's body inches from me and completely still, I could see how thin and gray his hair had gotten. I could see how pale his cheeks looked, almost completely colorless, despite the efforts of the funeral home makeup staff to give them some semblance of life. I could see how his hands, folded one on top of the other in the way those of dead bodies always are, now looked like boneless lumps of flesh, incapable of touching or grasping anything ever again. I could see my father not as a reflection of me—or as a reflection *on* me—but simply as he was. A man about to be put into the ground, Yosh was now completely and utterly harmless. There was no slight, no put-down, nothing he could do or say to hurt or embarrass me anymore.

Still, I waited for the tirade inside my head, the list of grievances, to start railing again. But as I stared at my father's lifeless form, all I could hear instead was his voice. Words I'd heard him say but never really listened to started to move in and out of my consciousness, like the fragments of light that sometimes flash or float by when your eyes are closed:

"Now, keep your nose clean" on the day I leave for college, as I slam shut the trunk of his Gran Torino and don't look back.

"You played a real good part" in the lobby of my high school auditorium.

"You need money?" while he holds out a crumpled twenty-dollar bill in one hand and hides his breakfast highball under the kitchen table with the other.

"John, I'm gonna buy you a drink" when I'm four years old, and he's recounting the story of how we knocked 'em dead with our traveling game show at Club Royale.

They were only words—snippets, fragments of a few stories from my one-eighth share of his life as a father and my one and only life as a son. And then they stopped. I was twenty-nine years old again, kneeling at his coffin, noticing how much the shape of his jaw looked like mine. Suddenly I was self-conscious, embarrassed, worried I had stayed too long. How long had I been there? I turned away, and tears were streaming down my face for the first time in seventeen years.

When I got up from the kneeling pad, my eyes met Kathy's. I wondered if she'd been watching me the whole time. A crier under everyday circumstances, Kathy was raccoon-eyed by this point, her face already a Rorschach blot of mascara. Without our thinking about it or saying a word, we embraced, tears now pouring out of me and onto Kathy's shoulder for reasons I didn't understand. I still don't.

Then the doors were open for the other mourners, and I took my place in the front line of the viewing room, my siblings and I all standing in a row. I don't know for sure if we were in birth order this time either, but that's the way I remember it. George, Donna, Larry, Nancy, Kathy, Benny, Michael, Thomas. At George's cue, we took one another's hands. We were all crying—maybe for our father's imperfect life, maybe for our mother's, too. Maybe for each of our fractured childhoods, which were now, at the same moment, slipping into the irretrievable past. It was the end of so many things. But it also felt like the beginning of something. Or maybe that's just the way I think of it now.

At the cemetery, I cried harder than any of my siblings, probably harder than anyone else at the funeral—loud, choking sobs from the center my chest—still without comprehension of what I was feeling or why.

As we headed back to our cars, my eyes caught those of Elaine, the woman with whom my father had shared the last seventeen years of his life. Barely able to get the words out, I said, "You made him so happy." I meant it sincerely, and I was completely taken aback by how much it mattered to me.

"Your daddy was always so proud of you kids," she said. I fell onto Elaine's shoulder and sobbed harder still.

~

After the funeral, we drove past our house on Lincoln Avenue, now owned and painted a different color by another family, and past the pigeon coop, still standing at this point but now birdless, just an oversized storage shed. We then continued three doors down to the American Legion hall for the repast. We ate lasagna and baked ziti served in aluminum foil trays, because it was a funeral in central Jersey, and kielbasa and pierogies, because it was a Polish funeral in central Jersey.

Adjacent to the banquet hall where we all gathered was the Legion's barroom, where my father had spent so many hours during my childhood: the night he staggered home and said he didn't give a goddamn if my mother died—and then she did—the night he introduced my brothers and me to Elaine while my mother sat in the next room, just weeks from her deathbed.

I took a few steps into the bar, a place I knew I would never see again, and peered through the gray, smoky air, which was illuminated only by a few dim, reddish lighting fixtures and signs for brands like Budweiser, Coors, and Seagram's 7. I breathed in the scent of stale booze, secondhand smoke, and wet cork that hadn't changed since my father's and my beer joint days when I was four.

"Want a drink?" asked Thomas, who I didn't realize had followed me. He was twenty-four years old now.

"Yeah," I answered involuntarily, as if it were the only possible answer to Thomas's question.

We pulled up a couple of stools and ordered two rye and ginger highballs, Yosh's cocktail of choice. We were the youngest people at the bar and probably the only two nonveterans in the room. I wondered if the bartender would question us, ask these two unfamiliar young men in dress shirts and loosened neckties who we were and whether we were members. But instead he just gave us our highballs, took our money, and walked away. I wanted to ask him if he had known John Sadowski, but I figured the chances were slim. I was pretty sure it had been a long time since Yosh had been at the Legion hall. My father was seventy-three when he died. He hadn't lived down the street on Lincoln Avenue in years, and by this point he'd probably been doing most of his drinking in secret at Elaine's house.

Thomas and I toasted our father with sentimental words I don't remember and lifted our glasses. Though I rarely drank whiskey, the fizz smelled familiar and sweet. As it hit my tongue, I didn't think about the crushing hold alcohol had had on my father's life or the destruction it had wrought on my mother's. I didn't think about the chaos my father's drinking and his disappearances into rooms like this had created for us kids. I didn't think about the time I fell asleep on the El after having had too much to drink myself or the time I woke up in a stranger's hotel room without remembering what had happened the night before. I didn't think at all about my life in Chicago or the fact that it was about to end with no real plan for what was next other than a U-Haul and a rented room in Hell's Kitchen.

All that mattered for the fifteen minutes I sat with Thomas at the American Legion bar was being in that room, and being there with my brother. We were two sons of a Legionnaire, and for a moment I felt—in a way I hadn't in a very long time—like I belonged.

AFTER

Man Walking

In the days that followed Yosh's funeral, Benny flew back to Atlanta, George drove back to Pennsylvania, and the others returned to their families in various parts of New Jersey while I prepared for my final weeks in Chicago.

Before I left Somerville, I visited Aunt Helen at the hospital, knowing it would probably be the last time I'd ever see her alive. Already gray and just a few weeks from death, she glanced up and brightened a little when she noticed me standing at the side of her bed.

"Hey! Whadda you doin' in here?" she asked faintly, with a hint of a smile. Then, offering some of her old routine with the small amount of breath she had left, she added with a weak finger wag, "You betta stop it!" It was a line she had used with us kids for years whenever we teased her about anything, like losing at bingo all the time.

"No, *you* betta stop it," I retorted. "You betta come home so you can make spaghetti and meatballs for us. Nobody makes it as good as you."

"Yeah," she said, trying to smile a little more.

I left Helen's room, took the elevator down to the lobby, then walked out into the hospital parking lot, from which a slice of Lincoln Avenue was visible in the distance. Once I passed all the cars clustered near the entrance and was far enough away from anyone who might hear, I stood in the blazing August sun and wept, as fully and loudly as I had at my father's grave. Then I went to the airport, boarded the return leg of my bereavement-fare flight, and flew to Chicago, where I wept again. And again.

The next part of my life was about to begin, yet I had no roadmap, no sense at all what was next. I had no job, no relationship, no idea if I was going to continue to pursue acting or do something else once I was back in New York. All I knew was that I was getting into a U-Haul and heading east.

I didn't know that, within three weeks of returning to New York, I would meet Robb, the person with whom I would spend the rest of my life. I didn't know that Robb would tell me, every day for twenty-nine years and counting, that he loved me and that I would believe it. I didn't know that I would never take that acting class, never go to another audition. I had no idea I would ever have the nerve to apply to a doctoral program at Harvard—or that they would actually accept me—and that Robb, his mother, and all of my sisters would cheer at my graduation. I didn't know that Yosh's prediction would come true and that someday I would become a professor—and write books and articles about queer teenagers and the relationships that save them from self-destruction.

I certainly never dreamed that Robb and I would be one of the first same-sex couples in the United States to become legally married, that Donna, Nancy, and Kathy would perform a reading at our Cape Cod wedding, or that George would offer the blessing before dinner while everyone in the room held hands.

I didn't know that someday my siblings and I would sign off our phone calls with "love you" and that I would believe that, too. Nor did I know that we would often group-text old photographs and memories of my parents, especially my father. We would crack up about Yosh's catch-phrases, the pigeon coop, sometimes even his drinking:

BENNY (on Yosh's birthday): This Day in History: 98 years ago today, shares of Fleischmann's Whiskey rise on anticipation of strong future sales.
KATHY: Good one, Ben!
NANCY: LOL

I didn't know that I would see Elaine again almost twenty-five years to the day after my father's funeral and that I would finally come out to her. She would say she was happy for me, then insist on giving me a snack for the ride home.

I didn't know that I would go to my twenty-five-year reunion at Northwestern, hardly know a soul, and sob. Then I would realize I was crying not because I felt alone there all over again but because I knew that the next day, I could go home.

I didn't know that all this could happen yet still not be enough to get rid of the old voices. I didn't know that, well into my fifties, they would still be here, lying in wait like Sheila Feldman behind the bushes at Van Derveer Elementary School. They would take whatever opportunity they could—a word, a look, or even just a long, dark night—to pull me down again and shame me into silence. And I didn't know that—most of the time, at least—I would get up and keep walking.

Acknowledgments

The term posttraumatic stress disorder (PTSD) did not appear in the American Psychiatric Association's *Diagnostic and Statistical Manual of Mental Disorders* until 1980 and was first used to describe the experiences of veterans who had returned from the Vietnam War. Prior to this, terms like "shell shock" and "battle fatigue" were sometimes used for similar phenomena among veterans of earlier wars, but it wasn't until the post–Vietnam War era that PTSD was widely recognized as a serious risk to the mental health of soldiers upon their return to civilian life.

I will never know if my father would have been diagnosed with PTSD had he performed his military service in a later decade, whether it played any significant role in his addictive behaviors or suicidal thoughts, or if he had any of the other manifestations such as nightmares, flashbacks, or the emotional triggering associated with the disorder. But I do know that some of his war experiences were harrowing: parachuting into active battlefields, being shot at, shooting and killing. So as much as this book is about the trauma of toxic masculinity norms, homophobia, and self-silencing, it's also about the traumas that come from war and alcoholism. And it's a story about the power of human connection and the bonding of a family in the face of trauma, in spite of everything.

My parents, as shown in the pages of this book, did not have easy lives and, like all parents, made their share of mistakes. But they also raised me and the seven other loving and successful people who are depicted in this story and to whom it is dedicated. To my sisters and brothers, I know there are some painful stories told in these pages, stories we would prefer not to remember. I think our collective experience growing up as Sophie and Yosh's children—both the good and the bad—are the reason we're the people we are today. So to both my siblings and my parents, thank you for our loving, supportive, and often crazy (in the best ways) family. It is one of the primary foundations of my life.

The other primary foundation of my life is my husband, Robb Fessler. To you I owe nothing less than my survival. I know your belief in me is the reason I'm still here, the reason I have the courage to write, the reason I have the confidence to think—even if it's only some of the time (old habits die hard)—that my story is worth telling. You are my best reader and my best friend. Every day, the look in your eyes and the sound of your voice keep me going. They are everything to me.

To Domenica Ruta, this book would not exist without you either. From the moment I set foot in your workshop at Gotham Writers in 2014, I knew you were the guide I needed on this journey. You were that rare and precious person every writer should have, the one who hears your voice and pushes you to be no one but yourself. For the years of coaching, editing, encouraging, answering all my nervous emails and texts about the business—and for your friendship—these words are not enough, but I hope the book is.

To Kelly Caldwell at Gotham Writers, thank you for your being a wonderful teacher who brought my work to the next level. Your voice rang in my head at so many moments through the writing process, and your influence is all over these pages. Thanks, too, for always cheering on my work, for always making time for me, and for your leadership of the best damn writing workshop in New York.

To the members of the Maiden Lane Writers Group—Marty Brown, Megan Gillin-Schwartz, Matthew Janes, Warren Shaw, Delia Springstubb, and Julia Wilson—your feedback and fellowship have been the fuel that has kept me going all the way to the final draft. The stack of all your comments that still sits next to my desk even as this book goes into production are a testament to the influence your wise, generous, critical readings of my work have had on the finished product. I'm so fortunate to have you as my writing home.

To psychologist Carol Gilligan, whom I had the privilege of working with in graduate school, thank you for your brilliant writings and ideas about gender, voice, and relationship, which run as an undercurrent through this entire book and so much else I have written. I would not have understood my story, or possibly even my life, without them.

To Heidi Kelleher, thank you for being the first teacher who encouraged me to write, and for generously reading this manuscript more than forty years later. If that's not a lesson about the enduring power of teaching, I don't know what is.

To my agent, Joelle Delbourgo, thank you for your keen understanding of the business, for your always savvy advice, for believing in this book in spite of the morale-killing market for memoir, and for not giving up even at moments when I almost did. This is very much your book, too.

To Nathan MacBrien at the University of Wisconsin Press, thank you for your unflagging enthusiasm about this project and for reminding me of the humor in it. And thanks for guiding it through the acquisition and production processes with a professionalism every author should be so lucky to experience. And to the entire team at University of Wisconsin Press—Jennifer Conn, MJ Devaney, Adam Mehring, Kaitlin Svabek, Jackie Teoh, and any others I may have neglected to mention—thanks for all your great work on behalf of this book and for being such kind human beings in our otherwise distant, newly remote world.

Finally, my deepest thanks to all the friends and family members who read early drafts, celebrated milestones with me, advised me about the business, dragged me kicking and screaming into social media self-promotion, gave me writing workshop sessions as gifts, or otherwise helped me navigate this long and sometimes difficult journey: Patricia Acha, Dani Almany, Tara Anderson, John Benscoter, Melinda Blitzer, David Downs, Audrey Fessler, Elsie Fessler, Amy Frank, John Manzo, Adam Troisi, Jefford Vahlbusch, and all my brothers and sisters. Young Michael may have had his trials, but older Michael has a lot to be grateful for.

Sources

Carol Gilligan, *In a Different Voice: Psychological Theory and Women's Development* (Cambridge, MA: Harvard University Press, 1993), xvi.

Henry Wadsworth Longfellow, "My Lost Youth" (1858), https://poets .org/poem/my-lost-youth.

Ricardo Piglia, *The Absent City*, translated by Sergio Waisman (Durham, NC: Duke University Press, 2000), 110.

Adrienne Rich, "Invisibility in Academe," in *Blood, Bread and Poetry: Selected Prose 1979–1985* (New York: Norton, 1994), 199 (part 1 epigraph).

Adrienne Rich, "Women and Honor: Some Notes on Lying," in *On Lies, Secrets, and Silence: Selected Prose 1966–1978* (New York: Norton, 1979), 186 (part 2 epigraph).

⁓

"Fascination," words and music by Ada Richter, Marie Pentz, Maurice de Feraudy, and F. D. Marchetti. Copyright © 1965 WC Music Corp. All rights reserved. Used by permission of Alfred Music.

"Me and Mrs. Jones," words and music by Kenneth Gamble, Leon Huff, and Cary Gilbert. Copyright © 1972 (renewed), Warner-Tamerlane Publishing Corp. All rights reserved. Used by permission of Alfred Music.

LIVING OUT

Gay and Lesbian Autobiographies

DAVID BERGMAN, JOAN LARKIN, and RAPHAEL KADUSHIN,
Founding Editors

Midlife Queer: Autobiography of a Decade, 1971–1981
MARTIN DUBERMAN

Self-Made Woman: A Memoir
DENISE CHANTERELLE DUBOIS

The Black Penguin
ANDREW EVANS

The Man Who Would Marry Susan Sontag: And Other Intimate Literary Portraits of the Bohemian Era
EDWARD FIELD

Body, Remember: A Memoir
KENNY FRIES

In the Province of the Gods
KENNY FRIES

Travels in a Gay Nation: Portraits of LGBTQ Americans
PHILIP GAMBONE

Autobiography of My Hungers
RIGOBERTO GONZÁLEZ

What Drowns the Flowers in Your Mouth: A Memoir of Brotherhood
RIGOBERTO GONZÁLEZ

Widescreen Dreams: Growing Up Gay at the Movies
PATRICK E. HORRIGAN

The End of Being Known: A Memoir
MICHAEL KLEIN

Through the Door of Life: A Jewish Journey between Genders
JOY LADIN

The Last Deployment: How a Gay, Hammer-Swinging Twentysomething Survived a Year in Iraq
BRONSON LEMER

Eminent Maricones: Arenas, Lorca, Puig, and Me
JAIME MANRIQUE

Body Blows: Six Performances
TIM MILLER

1001 Beds: Performances, Essays, and Travels
TIM MILLER

Cleopatra's Wedding Present: Travels through Syria
ROBERT TEWDWR MOSS

Good Night, Beloved Comrade: The Letters of Denton Welch to Eric Oliver
Edited and with an introduction by DANIEL J. MURTAUGH

Taboo
BOYER RICKEL

Men I've Never Been
MICHAEL SADOWSKI

Secret Places: My Life in New York and New Guinea
TOBIAS SCHNEEBAUM

Wild Man
TOBIAS SCHNEEBAUM

Sex Talks to Girls: A Memoir
MAUREEN SEATON

Treehab: Tales from My Natural, Wild Life
BOB SMITH

The Change: My Great American, Postindustrial, Midlife Crisis Tour
LORI SODERLIND

Outbound: Finding a Man, Sailing an Ocean
WILLIAM STORANDT

Given Up for You: A Memoir of Love, Belonging, and Belief
ERIN O. WHITE